40 Treasured
Bible Verses

JAMES C. HOWELL

40 Treasured Bible Verses

A Devotional

WESTMINSTER
JOHN KNOX PRESS
LOUISVILLE · KENTUCKY

© 2011 James C. Howell

First edition

Published by Westminster John Knox Press
Louisville, Kentucky

11 12 13 14 15 16 17 18 19 20—10 9 8 7 6 5 4 3 2 1

Book design by Drew Stevens
Cover design by Night & Day Design
Cover illustration: © Frank van den Bergh/istockphoto.com

Library of Congress Cataloging-in-Publication Data

Howell, James C.
    40 treasured Bible verses : a devotional / James C. Howell. — 1st ed.
        p.   cm.
    ISBN 978-0-664-23653-3 (alk. paper)
    1. Bible—Meditations. I. Title.
    BS491.5.H7 2011
    242'.5—dc22

                                                                2010034953

CONTENTS

INTRODUCTION

How strange: a book titled *40 Treasured Bible Verses*! The little segmentation of the Bible familiar to us as a "verse" didn't even exist until the sixteenth century. And how often does the Bible suffer crude misreading because we lop off a verse and make it say whatever we want it to say?

Yet it seems Jesus was utterly familiar with what we'd call verses. In a pinch he would quote from memory an especially poignant sentence from God's Word, whether he was preaching his first sermon (Luke 4:18–19) or dying on the cross (Mark 15:34). For many years, humble Christians would "memorize" Bible verses, unforgettable treasures that shaped thinking and living, providing solace and a true compass in times of duress.

In this book, I have tried to talk about verses with the context and background in mind. The lunacy of this endeavor was selection. The publisher said, "Let's do forty." Seemed easy, until I got busy picking: this one belongs, and we must use that one, and here's one I didn't think about at first . . . and it didn't take me long to zoom well past forty. Perhaps such a quandary is inevitable, given the riches of God's Word.

So we begin. Read, share, reflect, have a conversation with others. And poke around to find your own favorite Bible verses.

1

JOHN 1:14

The Word became flesh, full of grace and truth.

The Gospel of John begins like the first notes of some grand symphony, or perhaps the first brushstrokes of a masterpiece on canvas, or the first words whispered to you when you were cradled in your mother's arms. "In the beginning was the Word. . . . And the Word became flesh . . . full of grace and truth." Who was Jesus? Was he born to Mary in Bethlehem? Had he always been? John 1 unlocks a mystery. The Word always was God. Somehow, the fellowship that is God, the intimate relationships of love that are God's heart, have always been, and will always be.

The poetic genius of this overture to John's Gospel is astonishing and moving. Even in our day, when words are cheap, strewn meaninglessly all over the place, words matter. John's words are beautiful, for they speak of the one true Beauty. This symphonic ballet of language tries to express the inexpressible. God's inner self, God's loving heart, God's eternal fellowship, spilling over and making a world, knowing full well that the

3

world would miss the point and would be downright recalcitrant in reply—but Love loves anyhow.

Ask anyone: What was the most beautiful moment in your life? At first, most people recall some spectacular sight they once photographed. But if they linger over the question, they arrive at some truly beautiful moment when words that matter were spoken. "I love you; will you marry me?" "I forgive you." "I am immensely proud of you." "I just learned that I am pregnant." Life is birthed through words.

God created everything effortlessly with a mere word. "Let there be light." Jesus is the primal utterance of God, the Word behind the words, framed in the heart of God before time, yet not content to be sequestered outside of time. David Bentley Hart has written elegantly of "the scandal of Christianity's origins, the great offense this new faith gave the gods of antiquity, and everything about it that pagan wisdom could neither comprehend nor abide: a God who . . . apparels himself in common human nature, in the form of a servant; who brings good news to those who suffer and victory to those who are as nothing; who dies like a slave and outcast without resistance; who penetrates to the very depths of hell in pursuit of those he loves; and who persists even after death not as a hero lifted up to Olympian glories, but in the company of peasants, breaking bread with them and offering them the solace of his wounds."[1]

We often think of the Word becoming flesh as an emptying: Christ, "though he was in the form of God, . . . emptied himself, taking the form of a servant" (Phil. 2:6–7). But this Word isn't a hollow vessel, an empty shell. The humanity of Jesus *is* full; it is Fullness. The emptying is not an emptying of grace. The Word made flesh *is* grace. The flesh is God's glory. Jesus was not merely pretending to be human; he really did enter into our flesh of weakness, mortality, pain. There is no other God, no other secret truth about God. Jesus' suffering was no aberration from the truly glorious nature of God. God's glorious nature *is* the suffering. The Word made flesh is quite full of grace and truth.

We live in a culture that cares little for truth. Everything is about what works, what sells, what "seems" true. We've been lied to enough that we are cynical about the possibility of truth. And yet truth matters. Truth is our best defense against evil. Truth is more than mere facts. The historian David McCullough said, "You can have all the facts imaginable and miss the truth, just as you can have facts missing or some wrong, and reach the larger truth. 'I hear all the notes, but I hear no music,' is the old piano teacher's complaint. There has to be music. The work of history . . . calls for mind and heart."[2]

What is this music for mind and heart—this "fullness" of grace and truth? Don't we innately crave fulfillment? We stuff something inside the gnawing emptiness we feel in our souls: busy-ness, things, alcohol. Is Jesus what fills the hollow place? Yes—but we must be careful not to idolize our own cravings. It is not the case that Jesus satisfies us with what we've always wanted. No one desired Jesus. His own people rejected him; he "dwelled" among us, but we did not even recognize him. "He had . . . no comeliness that we should look at him" (Isa. 53:2).

The Word tutors our desires; they are converted into something truer. God has something far richer in store for us than merely what we thought would do. What did I desire five minutes before I thought about Christ? I cannot recall, and I'm not sure I heard the screen door slam behind me as I rushed out to follow him. I did not know what to desire until the one with no comeliness, the one singular Beauty, became flesh and dwelt among us, the wonderfully true Word overflowing with grace.

2

⌒⌒⌒

MATTHEW 18:3

Unless you become like children, you will never enter the kingdom of heaven.

We sigh sweetly on hearing Jesus say, "Let the children come to me, and do not hinder them" (Matt. 19:14). But what could he mean by saying, "Unless you become like children, you will never enter the kingdom"? In 1538, Martin Luther, stressed by his rambunctious household of six children aged four to twelve, puzzled over this: "What was Jesus thinking? This is too much: must we become such idiots?"[1]

In Jesus' day, as in ours, children were thought of as preliminary people, as if marinating, little projects in the making. But Jesus not only welcomes them, but points to them and says adults have unwittingly been plummeting downhill into immaturity for years. Grab your plastic bucket and pail, climb the hill, and become a child if you want to be truly mature, if you want to know God.

Consider Charles Péguy's words: "You believe that children know nothing, and that parents and grown-up people know something. Well, I tell you it is the contrary. It is the parents, it is the grown-up people who know nothing. It is the children who know everything, for they know first innocence, which is everything."[2] Children are open, they have more questions than answers, they are receptive, their jaws drop in awe rather easily. Children are under no illusions of independence. They do not hide their treasures, and they share their toys. Their calendars are not yet filled, and they are not in a hurry. Children toddle and are rather inept, and require much mercy.

Yet we dare not romanticize childhood—and even some of the more grueling aspects of being around children can teach us about life with God. Children demand a response, and *now*. They brook no rivals for their attention. They aren't trying to please anybody in particular, and they speak their minds quite boldly. Children may evoke a gentleness, but they are not gentle themselves. Somehow God is like such children, with an impatient, imperious cry of *Now!* And the urgency of that "Now!" may apply flawlessly to a moral rule of thumb Christians and non-Christians can agree upon: the thought of any child suffering, being mistreated, or going hungry is simply intolerable, and so we must do something—now!

I wonder if Jesus, if he lived in our media-crazed culture, would urge us to become like children. We have unwittingly ruined childhood. Fawning over children, we segregate them into groups of other children and insist they engage in "age-appropriate" activities—meaning they are never exposed to adults, to learn how to become adults. Jesus might not mind that failure to learn to be an adult so much. I laugh when I think of what C. S. Lewis said when asked why he penned "children's literature."

> Critics who treat adult as a term of approval instead of a merely descriptive term, cannot be adult themselves. To be concerned about being grown up, to admire the grown up because it is grown up, to blush at the suspicion of being childish, these things are the marks of childhood and adolescence.[3]

But we have ruined childhood by thinking kids can become grown long before they are ready. Neil Postman wrote of the "disappearance of childhood."[4] Once upon a time, there were adult "secrets" which you only learned when you were old enough to handle them. But now there are no secrets at all, and Jesus cannot have meant that we should become like today's children, who know as much or more than older adults. Jesus surely intended a kind of naiveté in children, an innocence, a beautiful lack of awareness of the tawdry, complex nature of adult life.

Parents think of children as problems to be solved, as projects to be pursued, but children are mysteries to be loved.[5] God, in the same way, is not a problem I try to solve with my brain, God is not a project I must manage or control; God is a mystery, and I am to love God the way a child loves her mother.

Jesus' reminder that we are to become like children is lovely, humbling, hopeful. Hans Urs von Balthasar pointed out that "only the Christian religion, which in its essence is communicated by the eternal child of God, keeps alive in its believers the lifelong awareness of their being children, and therefore of having to ask and give thanks for things."[6]

How on earth can a crusty, haggard, busy adult "become like a child"? You aren't a victim as much as you think: You can clear your calendar. Spend time with children: watch them, get on the ground and play with them, ask them to show you a treasure, and you show them one too. Share your toys.

3

⁓⊙⊙⁓

2 CHRONICLES 20:12

We do not know what to do, but our eyes are upon thee.

T he books of 1 and 2 Chronicles can make for some arid
reading . . . but how lovely is this modest but utterly faithful
prayer! *"We do not know what to do, but our eyes are upon thee."*

A coalition of petty tyrants have marshaled their armies and
are marching in battle formation toward Israel's border. The
news comes to Israel's king, Jehoshaphat. Unlike modern politicians, who posture for the cameras and talk tough, Jehoshaphat
is described, quite understandably, as "fearful" (2 Chron. 20:3).
Instead of unleashing his chariots and bowmen, he urges the
whole nation to pray and to fast. And he says out loud what no
politician today could ever say and keep his or her job.

Instead of uttering some cocksure plan, the king humbly
admits, "We do not know what to do." How stunning is this?
If we are sober when we face difficulties, we also do not know
what to do. No simple answer presents itself. Sometimes we
seem trapped between alternatives, neither of which is promising. The frank admission of helplessness, of not knowing how

to solve our problems, is not resignation to disaster; my inability to solve my troubles is the opening God needs. If I do not know what to do, I am thrown upon the grace and mercy of God; my weakness is my dependence on God's promise.

So where do we look when fear has us by the throat? Can't we begin by simply naming fear for the nemesis it is? Not that all fear is bad: if I am crossing the road and a truck is bearing down on me, I should be afraid and skidaddle. But so much fear is irrational: we fear what might happen, or we get strangled by what has happened. In our post-911 world, fear rules; politicians and advertisers sneakily appeal to our dark, fearful side. Security trumps in over all other goods; we do not know what to do, but at least we can try to be safe. If there were no God, to be afraid, and to do the only reasonable thing (to stay as safe as possible), would make sense.

But there is a God. We may not know what to do, but we need not fear. "Our eyes are upon you, O Lord." Scott Bader-Saye's words tantalize us: "Our overwhelming fears need to be overwhelmed by bigger and better things."[1] Jehoshaphat's fears are overwhelmed by something bigger: "Our eyes are upon God." A holy host of saints and humble believers have tried precisely this strategy, "looking to Jesus the pioneer and perfecter of our faith" (Heb. 12:2). Not knowing what to do, in fact, is the posture of faith God needs and craves, the end to the illusion of our independence, the frank admission that God knows, and God can.

Many of my friends treasure Thomas Merton's wonderful prayer:

> My Lord God, I have no idea where I am going. I do not see the road ahead of me. I cannot know for certain where it will end. Nor do I really know myself, and the fact that I think I am following your will does not mean that I am actually doing so. But I believe that the desire to please you does in fact please you. And I hope I have that desire in all I am doing. I hope that I will never do anything apart from that desire. And I know that if I will do this you will lead me by

the right road though I may know nothing about it. Therefore will I trust you always, though I may seem to be lost and
in the shadow of death. I will not fear, for you are ever with
me and you will never leave me to face my perils alone.[2]

We do not know what to do. But our eyes are upon God.
We look to God, we maintain our focus, we are determined that
whatever happens we will not take our eyes off God. There is
plenty to fear. More often than we'd like to admit, we have no
idea what to do. But our eyes are upon God.

4

GENESIS 28:16

Surely the LORD is in this place; and I did not know it.

For someone out of the Bronze Age, Jacob leads a life that
sounds strangely modern: moving from place to place, wily
enough to know how to get ahead in business, from a fine family but at odds with his in-laws, wife, and brother, with plenty
of savoir faire, lacking in piety, harboring more questions than
answers about God.

Not one to be afraid of the dark, Jacob sleeps heavily one
night and has one of those dreams that is so palpable you wake
up feeling the real world is vague, and you want to rewind the
clock to get back into the dream. He sees—what is it?—a ladder? or (as many Hebrew translators insist) a "ramp"? stretch-
ing up, up, into heaven itself. And there are—who?—people?
no, angels?—climbing up, down, passing each other, this one
drawing close to earth, another disappearing into the clouds. . . .

And then Jacob wakes up. "Surely the LORD is in this place;
and I did not know it." He did not ask for the dream, he was
not praying for God to show up, he was not even pretending to

be pious. But he discovered that God was there. From whichever point on land he found himself, there was a vertical dimension he had not paid attention to: if I am standing, or sleeping, or walking, at work, playing, eating, on vacation, tangled in an argument, watching TV, jogging, kneeling in church, or misbehaving in my private time, God is there.

Nathanael, the disciple about whom we know just a handful of intriguing facts, was found by Jesus, who said, "I noticed you under the fig tree." What was he doing under the tree? Resting in the shade? Working? Confessing his sins? Jesus saw him, but he didn't notice Jesus at all. Then Jesus reminded him of Jacob at Bethel: "You will see heaven opened, and the angels of God ascending and descending upon the Son of man." Jacob was surprised by God in a place, Bethel, causing him to exclaim, "How awesome is this place!" (Gen. 28:17). Jesus is now Bethel, the ladder into heaven, the surprising presence. How awesome is this Jesus!

Our lack of awareness of God is lousy evidence that God is not there! Archbishop Oscar Romero, speaking to hurting, fearful Salvadorans feeling forsaken by God—on Good Friday, 1980!—said:

> God is not failing us when we don't feel his presence. Let's not say: God doesn't do what I pray for so much, and therefore I don't pray any more. God exists, and he exists even more, the farther you feel from him. God is closer to you when you think he is farther away and doesn't hear you. When you feel the anguished desire for God to come near because you don't feel him present, then God is very close to your anguish.[1]

For Romero, prayer's greatest merit is when we are faithful despite not feeling the Lord's presence; we are closer to God than we think. Even our efforts to pretend there is no God, or to find some corner where God does not notice, are laughably impotent. "Where can I go from your spirit?" (Ps. 139:7 NRSV).

The Lord can even be in a place, through a stranger, and we don't notice it. "Do not neglect to show hospitality to strangers, for thereby some have entertained angels unawares" (Heb. 13:2). Jacob's grandfather, Abraham, welcomed and fed three traveling strangers—who turned out to be angels bearing extraordinary news, the very hope Abraham and Sarah were desperate for. Angels in the Bible don't shelter us so much as they bring a fresh, vital word from God to us. Hospitality to an angel isn't merely being nice: God speaks to us through those to whom we are hospitable!

Wherever we go, God is there, out there, but in here too. Hans Urs von Balthasar wrote that each of us "is built like a tabernacle around a most sacred mystery. . . . But this sanctuary is neglected and forgotten, like an overgrown tomb or an attic choked with rubbish, and it needs an effort to clean it up and make it habitable. . . . But the room does not need to be built. It is already there."[2] And, realizing this, we might understand the profound solace Thomas Merton noticed in his soul: circumstances may be difficult, he may not be as good as he would like, sickness, loneliness, or peril might dog him, but the one thing he could always say to God was, "Wherever I am, O Lord, there you are loved."[3]

5

⁤⁤⁤⁤⁤⁤∞⁤∞

PSALM 118:24

This is the day which the LORD has made; let us rejoice and be glad in it.

The Christian life would be immeasurably enriched if, when the alarm clock tolls in the morning, you could hit the off button, swivel your feet to the floor, stand up, take a good breath, and say, "This is the day the Lord has made; let us rejoice and be glad in it"—and perhaps reiterate this most faithful thought throughout the day.

A day can feel onerous, or perhaps like a leaky sieve, minutes slipping away, too much to do, rushing. But God made the day. The sun comes up and sets because God planned it; there is a divine rhythm to life. Each day is a precious gift, not for you to consume or cram full, but to delight in God the giver of the day, to serve the God who gave you the time.

When I have read about Mother Teresa or John Wesley rising at 5 a.m. to pray for two hours before breakfast, I feel annoyed or indifferent. "I'm not a morning person!" The synapses in my brain don't fire before the second cup of coffee; with kids and early appointments, morning is the worst conceivable time to cram in a devotion.

If you can carve out significant time with God before the rush of the day, then good! But even if you aren't a "morning person," some simple habits might strangely transform (and calm down) the balance of the day. When you are first jostled from sleep, notice your very first breath — and say, "Thank you, Lord." The grace of God has added another day to your life; that breath is a divine gift. Focus your eyes, and reflect for a nanosecond on the gift of sight. Hear a cricket, taste the juice, look into the face of your roommate, spouse, child (or your own in the mirror) — and for a millisecond thank God for the beauty of that face (even if etched with a crease from the pillow or still devoid of makeup). Develop the habit of momentary gratitude for all the small details that make life worth getting out of bed.

Morning bears so many palpable expressions of God's grace. The freshening dew (Hos. 14:5), the fog lifting, Venus brilliant (Rev. 22:16), a bird chirping praise, darkness banished (2 Pet. 1:19). The women discovered Jesus' tomb empty at dawn, so every morning is a mini-Easter. In Arthur Miller's *After the Fall*, Quentin says: "Every morning when I awake I'm full of hope, I'm like a boy! For an instant, there's some unformed promise in the air. If I could corner that hope . . . and make it mine."[1]

How to make the hope of the new day mine? As you walk downstairs or back out of the driveway, whisper, "This is the day which the Lord has made; let us rejoice and be glad in it" (Ps. 118:24). However briefly, never start any day without praying, "Lord, use me today. Sharpen my vision so I may notice your presence." Mother Teresa urged us, "Try to feel the need for prayer often during the day."[2] Maybe we could pray, "Lord, remind me to pray today."

The Hebrew original of this verse might be translated, "This is the day on which the Lord has acted." When the original psalmist sang, "This is the day the Lord has made," he was thinking about the great day in Israel's history, Passover, the day when the Lord acted to deliver his people from bondage, to set them free. We celebrate the great days on which the Lord acted: Christmas, when God came down and became small, to show us his heart, to win our hearts; Easter, when God raised Jesus from the grave and nixed the grip of death; and, if we think about it, every day, today. God acted today. God made today. God is involved. So no matter what else seems to transpire, we have good cause to be glad.

Bonhoeffer was right: "The beginning of the day should not be oppressed with besetting concerns for the day's work. At the threshold of the new day stands the Lord who made it. All the darkness of the night retreats before the clear light of Jesus Christ. All unrest, all impurity, all care and anxiety flee before him. Therefore at the beginning of the day, let the first thought and the first word belong to him to whom our whole life belongs."[3]

6

⁓⤳⤳⁓

PSALM 121:3

[The Lord] who keeps you will not slumber.

T his is the day which the LORD has made" (Ps. 118:24) does
not come to an abrupt halt when the sun sets or the supper
dishes are cleared, or when you brush your teeth and put on
your pajamas. If we awaken to God and make ourselves available to God in the morning, then how do we notice God like a
tender mother tucking us away at the end of the day? Am I just
too weary to think of God? Is my head a little woozy? With cha-
grin, someone told me, "When I get in bed and try to pray, I just
fall asleep." How perfect—like a toddler nestled in dad's lap,
able to rest in cozy security, drifting off, held securely. As this
day the Lord has made draws the shutters, we rejoice and are
glad. "[The Lord] who keeps you will not slumber" (Ps. 121:3).

Every evening is a little Sabbath. You rest. Mercifully, the
so-called "bad day" does end. Perhaps when we pause to pray
at day's end, we realize there had been much to be grateful for—
but we'd missed it earlier. Mother Teresa made a lovely suggestion: at the end of the day, look at your hands and ask them

where they have been and what they have done. If you would be close to God, you rigorously assess the day you have just been given by God, and in the light of the all-consuming love of Jesus you notice the shadows: one hand did reach into the cookie jar, the other was merciful; one hand waved God off more than once, the other handed food to the hungry. Confession is the opposite of negative thinking. My passion is to love God with every fiber of my being, in each moment, tangibly—and so to ask, not "How do I feel about my day?" but "God, what is your read on my day?" is the most positive, healthy, hopeful, progressive thought conceivable.

And new life is conceived! Yes, I fell woefully short today—but I pray for the power to do better tomorrow, and I relax into my pillow, relishing the curious joy of being able to let it go, to enjoy living as a forgiven person.

And as a grateful person. No matter how exhausted you think you are, devote a few minutes to a highlight reel of the blessings of the day, however small, and the fog of tiredness will lift. You breathed, you ate, the dog curled up at your ankle, the tree swayed in the breeze, the church is still standing. Look at your hands, fold them, and be thankful. You can rest now, in the comfort that God is good, and it's not all up to you, and there is a tomorrow.

Isn't it odd that the day is only twenty-four hours? When stuffing my calendar, I might wish I had thirty-nine hours . . . but not really. God is merciful in allowing us a mere twenty-four, or else we'd kill ourselves. And how bizarre that God wired us so that up to one third of the twenty-four you miss entirely! Try as you might to be Atlas, hoisting the world on your shoulders, you can never get cocky, for you have to sleep, and in the dark, when your eyes are shut, God is holding the world up just fine without you.

This principle will hold tomorrow when the sun's up, too. What will the morning be like? There is that newness that will dawn, the sun will come up, a new day is even now sweeping across God's good earth. Somewhere, in some other time zone, it is already tomorrow morning. As we drift off to sleep, we may be sure the Lord does not slumber, and the morning hope, being prepared even as we are unaware, is not a lie, but God's sure promise.

The darkness and quiet of evening are calming, but perilous: things go bump in the night. If the morning sunrise is a little mini-Easter every day, then perhaps the sunset is a little mini-funeral every day. "Now I lay me down to sleep. . . . If I should die before I wake, I pray the Lord my soul to take." One night will be your last, and the only waking up left to do will be with the God who gave you today. Each night, rehearse for your eventual death, trusting yourself into God's hands. So pray every evening with Cardinal Newman: "O Lord, support us all the day long of this troublous life, until the shadows lengthen, and the evening comes, and the busy world is hushed, and the fever of life is over, and our work is done. Then, in your great mercy, grant us a safe lodging, a holy rest, and peace at last."[1]

7

PSALM 19:14

Let the words of my mouth and the meditation of my heart be acceptable in thy sight, O LORD, my rock and my redeemer.

If we are intrigued by what living with God all the time is like, we could begin by praying these lovely words—although they might haunt us a bit. When we chat at the water cooler or converse at a party, are the "words of my mouth acceptable to you, O Lord"? There's more here than avoiding cussing, and God isn't particularly impressed by a pious, sugary niceness in our words. How do we talk in a way that pleases God and makes sense, given our faith?

Talk is cheap, and our culture is precipitously sliding into ever more decadent talk. Politicians may be vicious, TV stars crass. Shouldn't Christians monitor what we hear, and not be drawn into babbling away like everybody else? "Sticks and stones may break my bones, but words will never hurt me"? Nonsense. Words tear down, they belittle. We want to use our words to build up, to encourage, to say things that are excellent, that are helpful to others.

The Christian knows when *not* to talk. Dietrich Bonhoeffer suggested that "we combat our evil thoughts most effectively if we absolutely refuse to allow them to be expressed in words."[1] James, the brother of Jesus, warned that "the tongue is a fire" (Jas. 3:6). Christians always tell the truth, although there are truths we keep to ourselves, for some brands of honesty are cruel.

We unwittingly declare our values through words, so to talk fawningly over the bogus values of our culture hardly pleases God. If researchers recorded your actual words over a year or two, what would they conclude really matters to you? Would they get a sense that God is in your life? or that you are kind? or compassionate? or virtuous (without being smug)? What is the tone of my talk? Is my talk (over many years) becoming more acceptable to God? or less?

We want to talk about God, but we may get tongue-tied. Will I sound like a fumbling first-year student of some foreign language, so meager is my faith? Or will I turn the volume up too high and scare somebody off if I tell what God said to me yesterday? With so much ridiculous, innocuous, manipulative chatter about God out there already, why add to the Lord's name being taken in vain? Actions speak louder than words, right? But we need to say something about God, with ample room for questions, doubts, wonderings, tears, and laughter! Dorothy Day said, "If I have achieved anything in my life, it is because I have not been embarrassed to talk about God."[2]

The Psalm mentions words before thoughts: "Let the words of my mouth and the meditation of my heart be acceptable." How often do we talk before we think? What about our thoughts? What goes on inside my head? and why? How do I react to what I see? What am I feeling inside? Is there a way of thinking, and feeling, that is pleasing to God (who gave me my brain and emotions in the first place)? Thomas Merton asked "What good does it do to say a few formal prayers to Him and then turn away and give all my mind and will to things, desiring what falls far short of Him? . . . The mind that is the prisoner of conventional ideas, and the will that is the captive of its own desire, cannot accept truth and supernatural desire."[3]

Paul acknowledged that "the mind of Christ" strikes the world as foolishness (1 Cor. 2:14–16); we seek that secret wisdom. How do I change my mind, and begin to think God's thoughts? How do I value what God values? and shudder over what mortifies God?

For my "meditations" to be "acceptable" in God's sight, some housecleaning (junk removal?) is required. I turn my head at the end of the day, bang it, and the clutter tumbles out, leaving a clearing for God's beautiful ideas and perspectives from the Bible and our worship to take up residence. I start to want what God wants; I stop craving what is not of God. I linger over thoughts that are holy, and flee those that are base.

You can't get the mind of Christ the way Frankenstein got a brain, by getting hooked up for some high-powered transfer. You have to go back to school, immersing yourself in God's words, reflecting on them, practicing them—and gradually "the meditations of my heart" become more "acceptable" to our Lord. That the Bible provides us with this prayer, "Let the words of my mouth and the meditation of my heart be acceptable in thy sight, O Lord," implies they just might be. The Lord would not invite us to pray what cannot be answered. And so we pray, we speak, we think, and the grace is that this humble oblation is most certainly acceptable.

8

DEUTERONOMY 6:4

Hear, O Israel: The LORD our God is one LORD; and you shall love the LORD your God with all your heart, and with all your soul, and with all your might.

These words (called the Shema) are the most sacred in all Judaism; Jews recite this passage (in Hebrew!) at the beginning and end of each day. When Jesus was asked to pinpoint the heart of all Scripture (Matt. 22:37), he turned here: "Love the Lord your God with all your heart, . . . soul, and . . . might."

What does God expect? ask for? long for? Love. God doesn't say you must be good, or obedient, or frightened, or flawless. God wants love. But before you breathe a sigh of relief, remember how all-consuming, downright scary, and yet wonderful love is—or at least is supposed to be. We have trivialized love into nothing more than a fleeting mood, an emotion that surges and subsides. But love is a commitment, determination, loyalty, action. It looks like obedience, but isn't. There is a tender kind of fear that keeps love passionate. Love strives to be flawless.

Notice that love is evidently the kind of thing that can be commanded: Love! You can, you must, you'll miss everything if you don't. The premise to this uncompromising urgency to love God is that God is **one**! We live as if there were many gods, a new deity around every corner. The garden-variety gods of our culture (money, things, pleasure) are many, but they only burrow out a larger hole in the soul than the one we'd hoped they would fill. There is only one God, and that is why God is to be loved, not tucked away in a closet.

Hear, O Israel: . . . you shall love the LORD your God. Love begins when we **hear**. How can you love if you will not listen? To love God, we stop and listen. We converse with God, not when we holler loudly, but when we get quiet, open the Bible, and listen — and love begins.

As if to press home the point that love is serious, and all-embracing, Moses adds that we love God **with**: *with all your heart*, not just in a convenient corner of your heart, but **all** your desire, your passion, your mind, how you think, what you value.

With all your soul: not just with some spiritual side of yourself, but with your very life! To love with your soul means to sacrifice, to part with what is precious to you, for God. And not merely a "willingness" to sacrifice: if I love, I sacrifice. I examine my life and start boxing up my valuables, my time, my lifestyle, all that I've been sheltering, and I offer it up to God — and God is loved.

*With all your **might***: not just the little bit of energy or the spare change you have left after you've checked everything off your to-do list. The Hebrew word *me'od* means strength, ability, and also our tangible goods. We increase our pledge, give to missions, donate not old junk we don't want but items we treasure; in our spare time we hammer, we mentor a struggling family — and God is loved.

How do we love, not just now when we have good intentions, but tomorrow, next month, always? *These words which I command you this day shall be upon your heart; and you shall teach them diligently to your children, and shall talk of them when you sit in your house, and when you walk by the way, and when you lie down, and when you rise. And you shall bind them as a sign upon your hand, and they shall be as frontlets between your eyes. And you shall write them on the doorposts of your house and on your gates.* (Deut. 6:6–9)

If we are to love God, the words of God must be a regular feature in our routine, always lurking in the back of our minds, figuring prominently in how we think and why we feel as we do.

Moses declares that God's words should be "taught diligently": the Hebrew word, *weshinnantam*, means "to sharpen." Life in our culture is a continuous erosion of the soul, so our hearts are dull. We need to regain the edge of an awareness of God.

We are to speak of God while sitting at home, while walking outside; how can the things of God become a natural topic of conversation? Can our last thought before falling to sleep be a prayer of gratitude, our first thought upon waking up a plea for God's guidance?

We need reminders: Moses encouraged the Israelites to bind God's words on their hands, between their eyes, and on the door jambs of houses. Through history, Jews have fashioned and worn phylacteries, little boxes containing Bible verses, on their forearms and heads. Jewish homes feature the mezuzzah, where a doorbell might be—a small container with Bible verses inside. Maybe we could mimic that in some way: print a key verse and carry it in your pocket, or stick it in your desk drawer. Hang a picture of St. Francis or Mother Teresa in your bedroom or den. Download a Scripture reading or hymn onto your iPod.

Unless we find very practical ways to be reminded of God, we drift into society's boring, consumer mindset, and we hardly ever think of God until there is a crisis. Love doesn't wait for a crisis. God is one, and we love God—with all.

Feb 23

9

⌒◯⌒

PHILIPPIANS 4:6

In everything by prayer and supplication with
thanksgiving let your requests be made known to God.

Through the worst depression conceivable, through grave
personal losses, through emotional wreckage and even the
darkest chapters in the annals of history, one solid rock endures:
we can let our requests be made known to God. God cares. God
does not manipulate events down here, but God is immensely
compassionate, God listens and stands ready to support.

How intriguing! Paul says, "With thanksgiving let your
requests be made known to God." Our usual pattern would be
to let our requests be made known to God, and then—*if* God
does what we ask—only *then* do we give thanks. Paul must be
inviting us to a very different place.

The very ability to pray, the brute fact that I am awake,
breathing, and capable of even a dim belief in God is an extraordinary gift for which to be thankful. Simply existing is under-
valued, isn't it? Without the gift of life, without the grace of God
that makes me bright enough to care, to fret, to lift my eyes to
God, or to hope, I would be like a worm or a stone.

Who deceived us into thinking thankfulness is about appreciating a nice house or sumptuous food, fine wine, or a vacation in the Rockies? Wasn't Jesus trying to teach gratitude when he said, "Do not lay up . . . treasures on earth, . . . but lay up for yourselves treasures in heaven" (Matt. 6:19–20)? Treasures in heaven we have in ample supply: God's mercy, the hope of blissful eternity, moral zeal, purpose and meaning, the wonder of salvation, our unshatterable relationship with saints, family and friends who have died, Jesus and the angels praying for us, the unfathomable riches of God's love and tender care.

And the blessings here are not diminished by a downturn in the economy: bodies that function, the way rain softens hard earth, the beauty of leaves in autumn, a child's laughter, the wrinkled smile on your grandmother's face, the nobility of people who rush to help one another, friends, family, shelter, the taste of water or a strawberry . . . and the church which, for all its foibles, remains the best hope of humanity to dream of goodness and to embody the love of God.

The delightful secret of making our requests known to God resides in doing so "with thanksgiving." We kneel, we close our eyes, we bow our heads, and we express our gratitude, and then we request, which rather wonderfully creates more reason for gratitude, and then more boldness in making requests, and thus more gratitude—and the circle feels like the arms of God enfolding us in an intimate embrace of love.

"In everything . . . with thanksgiving, let your requests be made known to God." Paul urges us to make our requests to God, with thanksgiving—but not just when we are in dire straits. Isaac Bashevis Singer said, "Whenever I am in trouble I pray. Since I am always in trouble, I pray all the time."[1] We pray with thanksgiving "in everything," at all times, in happy and tough circumstances, in the mood or not.

God's life with us touches everything: the chair in the den, the coffeepot, the photo album, the azalea bush, the calluses on my hand, the bit of talent in my head, my shrinking investment portfolio, the car, music, an apple on the counter, the pillow and my weary head upon it. God is obsessed with every detail of our lives, God cares about the things we sit on or forgot we had in the attic, God wishes to love us through everything, and for us to love God with everything.

"In everything . . . with thanksgiving, let your requests be made known to God." What might "everything" really include? Good things? What about bad things? Are we the best judges of what really is good or bad? Might we find ways to give thanks to God not so much for what we have accumulated, but even for what we may have lost? Wistfully I recall childhood stays with my grandparents; those days, and my grandparents, are long gone—but I am grateful.

We love, we lose, we shed tears and bear a deep ache in our souls. Are there ways to be grateful? What if there were no tears, no ache? Dietrich Bonhoeffer wrote a Christmas letter to his parents, not long before his own death:

> Nothing can make up for the absence of someone whom we love. That sounds hard, but at the same time it is a great consolation, for the gap, as long as it remains unfilled, preserves the bonds between us. It is nonsense to say that God fills the gap; he doesn't fill it, but keeps it empty and so helps us to keep alive our former communion with each other, even at the cost of pain. The dearer and richer our memories, the more difficult the separation. But gratitude changes the pangs of memory into a tranquil joy. The beauties of the past are borne, not as a thorn in the flesh, but as a precious gift.[2]

Indeed, in everything, with thanksgiving, we make our requests known to God.

10

2 CORINTHIANS 12:9

My grace is sufficient for you, for my power is made perfect in weakness.

Paul, always confident of enjoying direct access to Jesus in heaven, tells us that Jesus told him this: "My grace is sufficient for you, for my power is made perfect in weakness." How did Jesus say this to Paul? We do not know precisely.

Perfection in weakness is Jesus' entire story. God manifested his immense power, not by rumbling down from heaven with a horde of chariots, but as a tender, totally vulnerable infant, unable to walk or talk or do anything except simply be held by his mother. Jesus exhibited the kingdom of God by having no home or possessions: "Foxes have holes, and birds . . . have nests; but the Son of Man has nowhere to lay his head." He became a laughingstock, rode a mere donkey instead of a stallion, was shackled and beaten; in an incredible show of weakness he did not even argue with Pilate, and spoke astonishing words of forgiveness over the very soldiers who had just nailed his frail body to a shaft of olive wood. But that moment was the perfect display of the heart of God, the ultimate embodiment of the truth about the universe, grace sufficient.

What an understatement: "My grace is sufficient"—as if it's just barely enough—it will suffice, it'll do. Oh, no—the grace is overwhelmingly more than enough; an embarrassment of riches floods my soul and God's redeemed world in the weakness of Christ's love. Carried on the tide of such a deluge of grace, I do not need to mask my weakness ever again. "My richest gain I count but loss, and pour contempt on all my pride." God's power happens when and where I have nothing but weakness to plaster on my résumé, applying for holy grace.

How perfect is this for you and me! We live in a world that despises or cloaks weakness; we play to strength, we value success. But in the Gospel's upside-down logic, weakness is good. It's not that the strong are doomed! Rather, the secret is acknowledging our weakness. I am vulnerable, unable to achieve what I most need in life; I am needy, mortal, uncertain—no matter how nimbly I erect a facade of having it all together. Martin Luther said that "faith is the humility that turns its back on its own reason and strength."[1] So weakness isn't a problem God helps me overcome: this is the opening for God to be God, to lift me up, to be great in me, in spite of me. "Jesus loves me! This I know . . . ; Little ones to Him belong"—and when I admit I am little, then I take hope: "They are weak, but He is strong."

When I am weak, when I am needy, when I let the truth about me be exposed, then God takes me by the hand. It is God's strength, not mine; God's unfathomable ability, not my meager attempts; God's marvelous grace, not my feeble stab at doing a little bit of good, that matters. Paul says God's strength is "made perfect" in weakness. The Greek verb *teleitai* means "bring to completion" or "made fully present." When I am weak, God's grace, God's unmerited, unstinting love for me, for us, is complete, no longer blockaded by my ego, by my titanic attempts to manage my own life; God is present, God is good, God is gracious.

Once there was a boy born with an acute case of cerebral palsy, who was treated terribly as a young child, and then went to another home where his new mother noticed how he watched *Mister Rogers' Neighborhood*. She believed Mister Rogers was keeping her son alive. Some foundation worked it out for Mister Rogers to visit this boy, and when he did Mister Rogers asked, "Would you pray for me?" The boy was thunderstruck because nobody had ever asked him for anything. He had been the object of prayer, not the one to pray for anybody. But he began to pray for Mister Rogers and didn't want to die anymore. A journalist, Tom Junod, witnessed this and privately congratulated Mister Rogers for being so smart. But Mister Rogers didn't know what he meant. He really wanted the boy's prayers, saying, "I think that anyone who's gone through challenges like that must be very close to God."[2] They are weak, but he is strong. "The Spirit helps us in our weakness, . . . we do not know how to pray . . . , but the Spirit . . . intercedes for us with sighs too deep for words" (Rom. 8:26).

In the Roman world in which Paul wrote "My power is made perfect in weakness," critics mocked Christianity as a religion for weaklings. Indeed.

11

PSALM 46:10

Be still, and know that I am God.

So we want to expand our spiritual horizons, to probe the depths of God's heart, to be better. For any of this to happen, we have to stop.

For most of us, our lives are like some overloaded train rambling out of control. But instead of applying the brakes, we frantically shove more coal into the engine, going faster, taking on more cargo, rushing toward . . . well, we aren't sure at all where we're going. To be remotely serious about the Christian life, you have to stop, or leap from the train if you have to, scrape your knees and elbows, then stand, dust yourself off, and be still.

"Be still, and know that I am God"—and I've always thought the psalmist should have added, " . . . and you aren't." I am not God, and you aren't either. God can handle being God just fine; I'm freed from that burden. Society says, "It's all up to you—so hurry, cram, grab, more, more, more." No wonder we're tired. No wonder we feel empty: we aren't empty at all, just full of too much junk, too much rushing around, too much of the fiction that "it's all up to me." Like Sisyphus, we feel condemned forever to push a huge rock uphill all day long, only to get near the top but have it roll back down, and the next day, we go at it again.

Jesus said, "Come to me, all you who labor and are heavy-laden, and I will give you rest" (Matt. 11:28). God's greatest gift is that we can be still, and it will be OK. Life is not finally measured by my frantic, energetic bursts to make something happen that will fill the void. Grace is no more or less than this: the world is in the hands of God, and I can just back off, be still, and know that God really is God.

Being still is hard, countercultural, downright agonizing. We are addicted to stress. We keep moving, and if we ever do stop, we are tireder than we thought we were, and we sense a need to get moving again. But who says, "Keep moving, go faster"? It is not our Lord, but the voices of a culture far too harried to know the living God.

Growing up in his boyhood home that doubled as his family's business, Jesus would have learned this verse from his parents: "Be still, and know that I am God" (Ps. 46:10). The disciples, to our knowledge, never asked Jesus, "Lord, teach us how to manage our time more effectively and get more messianic acts accomplished." They did ask Jesus, "Lord, teach us to pray." Jesus had a rather notable habit of slipping off by himself, not to recharge his batteries or to get in some R & R, but to be with God, to be still. "Jesus went up on a mountain by himself to pray." When the disciples saw Jesus' intimacy with God, they wanted in on the best thing they'd ever laid eyes on.

And so might we—but to understand even the subtle hints of such an intimacy, we need to look hard at the lie at the heart of our society that Jesus would expose: that more is better, that rushing here and there is the path to life, that if we have done forty things each day we're better off than getting only four things done. What, after all, did Jesus say to the frazzled ("distracted") Martha? "You are anxious and troubled by many things, one thing is needful" (Luke 10:38–42).

To connect with God, we have to have the courage to slam on the brakes. Watch the house of cards tumble into a heap! But then the cards are all on the table, and we look across at God and see his tender, firm, loving face. God reaches across the messy table, takes your hand gently, strongly, and says, "Be still, and know that I am God." "But what am I supposed to do?" And God answers, "Nothing just yet. For now, be still. Get calm inside. Be with me for a while."

And be still, perhaps, with someone else. We think too blandly that stillness, or spirituality, is something that happens when I am alone. But it could be that God gave us good company to learn how to have solitude with God, to give each other the freedom to be still. Nicholas Lash spoke of the Church as a "school of stillness."[1] Somebody else is tired; somebody else needs to see that God has the world quite well under control. If you are reading this book, be assured others are too, somewhere, today, tonight. We enjoy an invisible, mysterious, but lovely fellowship of those who seek this God who frees us to be still. Together, we can be a school of stillness. Together we (who are not God) wait, we long, wondering what God will do. And God keeps speaking quietly but firmly, as the crowd of saints gather: "Be still, and know that I am God."

12

1 JOHN 1:1–2

That which was from the beginning, which we have heard,
which we have seen with our own eyes, and touched with
our hands, concerning the word of life — the life was made
manifest, and we saw it, and testify to it.

Real people, with dreams, flaws, wounds, and loves, were
eyewitnesses to events so profound, so transformative, that
their knees buckled, they blushed — and could not keep their
thrilling experience of God to themselves. At first, they blurted
their story out loud, a bit breathless; and then, after digesting
the full meaning and unanticipated consequences of what God
had done, they wrote it down to mail to others in distant lands,
and in future centuries — like us.

Is the Bible human? or is it divine? We believe it is both. How
else would God speak to us? And the whole point of the story
is that God entered into the vulnerability, pains, and delights
of human existence — so we expect the words about God to be
quite human.

We need human words. Golden tablets parachuted down
from heaven would never warm the heart. We crave the power
of human testimony: the sighs, emotions, and commitments elic-
ited when someone says, "I love you," "I promise . . . ," "We will

make it through together"—even if the speaker stumbles, says, "Uh . . . ," and has a fact or two a bit crossways. The Bible has its blemishes, as critics have never ceased to point out, and as its fans have never been reluctant to admit. God entered the messiness of humanity; God entrusted God's own self, and thus God's message, to human authors.

The Spirit of God was totally involved—but not as a drill sergeant. The Spirit kept holy, loving, nudging arms around the whole process of the Bible's composition and formation, the way a parent launches a toddler with wobbly legs, allowing a tumble or two, but ensuring the child finds balance and learns to walk, run, dance, and leap for joy.

To see how lovely the messiness of the Bible can be, look at verse 4 of this chapter: "We are writing this that our joy may be complete." The writers of the Bible were themselves seeking joy! But the word "our" might not be correct. In some early manuscripts we find the word "your": "We are writing this that *your* joy may be complete." I have no doubt that the writers who cobbled the Bible together believed that we who read would find joy in their words—that's why they wrote them. An uncertain text: but what a beautiful error, and we can spend eternity debating who was right, who got the most joy out of the Bible, its writers or its readers.

But the Bible is such an old book—can it still matter? God gave laws to Moses for the people to obey back in the Bronze Age; Isaiah called King Ahaz on the carpet in the eighth century BCE, and Jeremiah encouraged depressed exiles in the sixth; Paul dashed off a letter to the Corinthian Christians who were misbehaving about the year 54 CE.

Think of the writers of the United States Constitution. Madison, Morris, and their colleagues were dealing with eighteenth-century realities, but they laid down the basics that would forever define who we are as a people: we will have a representative government, we will never have a king, and so forth. The burden on the country will always be to apply those founding principles in changing epochs.

The Bible functions in the same way. Through its stories,

songs, laws, and letters, significant turf is staked out: the world belongs to God who made it, God expects us to be holy, Jesus is everything, we never tolerate poverty, and so forth. The Church's dogged existence across time is the proof that the book still works. But why? People are people. I am very much like Adam, Jacob, Peter, Dorcas, and sometimes Mary and Jesus himself; our shared humanity before the God who made us all invigorates the truth of this human Bible.

But perhaps more importantly, 1 John 1:3 says the story is told "so that you may have fellowship with us; and our fellowship is with the Father and with his Son Jesus Christ." The Church is not merely a building, but the people of God, enjoying a solidarity across space and time. We are the Body of Christ, and his book is our book, written long ago for the Church, copied, cherished and translated by the Church, always giving life, challenge, and hope to the Church then, now, and forever.

We speak of the Bible as "inspired"—and can we think not merely of writers but also of readers as moved and guided by God? Isn't this where the Holy Spirit does its most marvelous labor, lifting the words from the page and igniting something in the soul, so we might "get" the words and be transformed by them? The inspired Word seeks inspired readers.

Can we make the Bible relevant? Maybe the Bible simply *is* relevant, and the issue is whether we can make our lives relevant, whether we can recraft an existence that makes sense in light of our Constitution, the living Word God has graciously provided for our joy.

13

DANIEL 3:17–18

Our God whom we serve is able to deliver us from the
burning fiery furnace. But if not, be it known to you,
O king, that we will not serve your gods or worship the
golden image which you have set up.

Little children learn the story of Shadrach, Meshach, and Abednego, and perhaps they can sing (with the sizzle sound), "It's cool in the furnace." But the immense courage, the stalwart faith, of these three Israelites is for grownups, for those who dare to live boldly for God in the teeth of a glitzy world that fawns after shiny lies.

The setting is the impressive empire of ancient Babylon, featuring one of the "Seven Wonders"—the Hanging Gardens of Babylon. Israel boasted no such "wonders," as their one prize building, Solomon's Temple, lay in ruins. Israel had been crushed by Nebuchadnezzar's merciless army, Jerusalem reduced to rubble, and its citizens compelled to live in exile far from home.

The mighty king did what all potentates and societies do: he wanted unity, he required loyalty, he had a litmus test for whether you were with him or against him: a dizzyingly tall, opulent statue before which all were to bow down. Are you patriotic? Will you fit in here in Babylon? It's not hard to recall history's chronicle of political regimes that insist on obsequious support, that brook no dissent—and even cultures (like our own) that demand that you fit in, that you bow to the gods of this world, or you're an outcast.

Threatened with death by fire, Shadrach, Meshach, and Abednego make a startling declaration that must have offended and stunned the king: "Our God . . . is able to deliver us." Nebuchadnezzar must have snickered. Strong faith in the true God draws sneers in every age.

But notice what they say next—not "God will deliver us, so we aren't worried about your fire." Instead they say, "God *can* deliver us; but *even if he doesn't*, we will never, ever bow down." This is faith, true courage, and untouchable hope. No optimistic "Oh, because of God everything will turn out just fine" for them. They are fully prepared to bear whatever the cost to remain doggedly loyal to a God others disregard. Nothing can strike fear into their hearts or prompt them to a change of heart. The martyrs throughout history are our most stellar heroes, those making the ultimate sacrifice for their commitment to God.

Their miraculous rescue from the fire is almost anticlimactic after their stirring profession of faith. Nebuchadnezzar saw not three, but four men in the furnace . . . and then the three walked out: "the hair of their heads was not singed, . . . and no smell of fire had come upon them."

What is the depth of our faith? or the extent of our commitment to God? Do we merely "trust" God to shelter us from all harm? Or do we follow in the steps of Shadrach, Meshach, and Abednego—oh, and also Jesus, and Peter, and a holy host of saints and martyrs? We know God can do anything; but even if God does not work a miracle for us, even if we are ridiculed or even endangered, we will be steadfast in our refusal to bow down to the glittering images the world vaunts as the good life. We will never cave in, we will never smoothly fit in. As Jesus put it, perhaps thinking of this very story, "Do not fear those who kill the body but cannot kill the soul; rather fear him who can destroy both soul and body . . . [So] fear not . . . every one who acknowledges me before men, I also will acknowledge before my Father . . . in heaven" (Matt. 10:28–32).

In the catacomb of Priscilla in Rome, one of the simplistic but theologically profound colored paintings scrawled on the wall is an image of Shadrach, Meshach, and Abednego, flames darting about their feet — and yet they almost appear to be dancing, gleeful, or at least still alive. Christians huddled in those ancient stone burial chambers to be near friends and family who had died and to the God they knew had delivered them through the fires of death and persecution into heaven. In those days, to live and die as a Christian was quite literally a matter of life and death. To them, following Christ wasn't identical to having a pulse. You had to say to the Roman Empire, and to the Roman economy, and even to ridiculing neighbors and family members, "God can deliver us, but even if he doesn't, we will never bow down." As they prayed, and praised, they took heart from the three young men of Babylon who were never for one instant alone in that furnace.

14

ROMANS 12:2

Do not be conformed to this world, but be transformed by the renewal of your mind, that you may prove what is the will of God.

Sometimes Christianity feels like a kind of dull conformity, a rigid grid of rules that makes us shiver. But there is more than enough conformity out in the world! Society shouts at us to fit in; we learn our cues, we mimic, we shop.

Rather wonderfully, Paul urges us: "Do not be conformed to this world." Life with God is not conformity; the life of faith is "transformation." The Greek word is *metamorphōsis*—the near miraculous process by which a grayish brown pouch is "transformed," and a colorful butterfly takes flight. The power of God is like that: not cramming us into a hard shell with no wiggle room, but setting us free so we might soar and discover beauty. We revel in the unique creature God made each one of us to be; God's vision for me, and for you, is special.

The Spirit's work is a "renewed mind." Our minds get stuck in a hardened rut, but then God peels away the old patterns of thought and our imaginations are set on fire. We think God's thoughts, we seek "the mind of Christ" (Phil. 2:5); we put on the spectacles of God's Word and see the world and people from God's perspective. This renewed mind is a great joy, but pain is involved. Bob Pierce, the founder of World Vision, said, "Let my heart be broken by the things that break the heart of God."[1] We befriend the poor, we weep over the sorrows of the world, we hold today's grief very close to the hope of a new day, and then we are near to the heart of God.

We begin to know God's will, and we let it happen. In a world that endlessly debates the will of God, we who are transformed by God simply go out and do it—we trust it. We "prove" the will of God by embodying what Paul spoke of in the verse leading up to this one: "I appeal to you . . . , by the mercies of God, to present your bodies as a living sacrifice, holy and acceptable to God, which is your spiritual worship" (Rom. 12:1). The secret to transformation, morphing from the cocoon of a "normal" life to the colorful beauty of life with God, is worship.

Worship, at least in this verse from Paul, is not a sequence of motions you go through in a sanctuary. Worship is when we "present [our] bodies as a living sacrifice." We attend worship, we enter into it humbly and eagerly—but then we seek the new posture out in the world, a passion of the soul to offer up who I am, all I have, my full-bodied existence, to God. I am not my own; I am entirely God's property.

In Bible times, you took your best lamb, or the first wheat that ripened, and you laid it on the altar and let the priest set it on fire—a sign that what belongs to you doesn't really belong to you at all, but to God. And once it's sacrificed, you can't get it back: the smoke curls up toward God, who is pleased. If you and I could think of our lives (body, time, possessions) as not belonging to us, but entirely to God, liberated from the need to cling, imagine how richly fulfilling our lives might be! To avoid God, to shut ourselves to the Spirit, is to cower in the cocoon and refuse to fly. To open ourselves to God, to be transformed, is the most exhilarating delight—and the whole world is the beneficiary.

In our culture, obsessed with consuming, we need to weigh the virtue of ridding ourselves of something precious. Reflect on Eugene Peterson's wise words:

> Sacrifice exposes spiritual fantasy as a masquerade of faith. Sacrifice scraps any illusion, no matter how pious, that is spun by the devil. Sacrifice plucks out the avaricious eye. Sacrifice lops off the grasping hand. Sacrifice is a readiness to interrupt whatever we are doing and build an altar, bind whatever we happen to be carrying with us at the moment, place it on the altar, and see what God wills to do with it.[2]

Even puzzling moral quandaries seem simpler when we think of life as worship. My body, my time, my stuff, my abilities, this decision, that spare hour: all are God's, all are my pleasure to hand over to God. "Take my life, and let it be consecrated, Lord, to Thee."

Then (and only then!) comes the transformation. God takes what I offer and makes it holy, placing it meaningfully into the plot of God's adventure on earth; and my life becomes a thing of beauty in God's eyes. The world may scratch its head and wonder, but then the world might also be drawn to me, to the Church, to God. For instead of a convenient, superficial Christianity, the real thing will be in evidence — and we believe that a life devoted to God is lovely, alluring, persuasive.

15

JOHN 21:15

*When they had finished breakfast, Jesus said to Simon
Peter, "Do you love me more than these?" He said to him,
"Yes, Lord; you know that I love you." He said to him,
"Feed my lambs."*

Jesus asks, "Do you love me?" not once but three times — but
why? We do not know. What does Jesus mean when he
adds "more than these": Do you love me more than these what?
More than the fishing boat, the nets, the way of life Peter relied
on? More than the other disciples love Jesus? Wouldn't Jesus
want us to avoid comparing our faith to others and realize we
love Jesus together with others?

Do you love me "more than these"? Might he mean the blessings God gives? We love what God gives us, but do we love
God? Is God merely the one we hold at bay as long as we get the
good things we want from God? Doesn't God want our time,
our hearts, our selves — the way a parent wants to be loved,
instead of being the dispenser of cash on demand?

Maggie Ross once wrote that there are people who prefer an
"experience" of God over God himself.[1] We want the feeling,
the warm rush of emotion — but isn't a substantial relationship
with God more than something we experience inside ourselves?

Shouldn't our faith be about God, not just me and my religious emotions? Can we stick close to God during stretches of time when the feelings have subsided?

Peter insists that he does love Jesus. We wish we could see Jesus' face: Did he smile? nod? raise an eyebrow? extend his arms? We know his next words, though: "Feed my sheep." If we claim we love God, if we even wish to love God, it involves feeding God's sheep, caring for those who are lost, hungry, and thirsty.

John 21 uses an unusual, theologically profound Greek word: *agapē*, which is a love deeper than what we feel for family and friends, beyond simple liking or affection. This love, *agapē*, is eager to love the unlovable, the stranger nobody else will attend to, even my enemy. This divine love, *agapē*, does not bubble up spontaneously in the soul. It must be learned; a healing must happen. We pray for the miracle of God's Spirit to love through us and in spite of us with the *agapē* with which Jesus loves us.

But let's reconsider this moment hanging in time: "When they had finished breakfast, Jesus said to Simon Peter, . . . 'Do you love me more than these?'" At first blush, we assume this question is designed to reveal the heart of Peter (the one who must answer); but maybe it tells us more about Jesus than about Peter, more about God than about us (who must answer today). If Jesus asks "Do you love me?" it must be that Jesus wonders, that Jesus is intrigued by what is in our hearts, that Jesus wants something more than intellectual interest or distant admiration.

Or even our good, charitable works. I hammer on the Habitat house, send prayer cards to a shut-in, tutor once a month, drive the youth on mission trips, put money in the plate, serve a meal at the homeless shelter now and then. Isn't that what Jesus had in mind? Yes, of course; Jesus did tell Peter to "feed my lambs." But he asked not once, but three times, "Do you love me?" Isn't my service résumé sufficient to pass muster as "love" for Jesus?

In *Fiddler on the Roof*, Tevye (the "papa" of grown daughters) surprises his wife, Golde, by asking, "Do you love me?" She shakes her head and replies, "For twenty-five years I've washed your clothes, cooked your meals, given you children. . . . Why talk about love now?" But he persists, "Do you love me?" We may do things for God, serve in the church, refrain from immortality, study our Bibles: all good, outward expressions (perhaps!?) of an inward love. But Jesus, like Tevye, presses us: "Do you love me?"

How would we love? Belief is hard enough. God doesn't pop out in the open so we can embrace God or wrap up a present to show our love. But it is good to know that the goal, the relationship sought on God's side, is love, not servility, not nice behavior or intellectual banter, but something close, personal.

What might draw us into love with Jesus? In our relationships who is more vulnerable, the one who asks, "Do you love me?" or the one who is asked? If you ask, you are vulnerable, because the one asked might look away, or the one loved might not love in return—which is crushing to the one who loves and has risked everything by asking. Jesus puts himself in the vulnerable position—which God has always done, no matter how much we fancy God as all-powerful and all-controlling. Jesus loves; God takes the risk of vulnerability, bearing the possibility of rejection, because God loves, and "love does not insist on its own way" (1 Cor. 13:5). Vulnerable Love incarnate loves us enough to come down and risk whether we love in return, or not. How will we answer the only question that matters: "Do you love me?"

16

PSALM 23:4

Even though I walk through the valley of the shadow of death, I fear no evil; for thou art with me; thy rod and thy staff, they comfort me.

The Twenty-third Psalm is a spiritual rock star. Yet, for all its familiarity there may be some nuances we've missed. Consider one four-letter word in verse 4: "thou"—old English, a relic from the 1611 King James Version. Usually we prefer modern translations, but Christians cling to a four-hundred-year-old translation of Psalm 23. Why? Could it be that elevated language, words with lineage and dignity, are appropriate to the grandeur, the majesty, the immeasurable grace of God, who is our shepherd?

Thou. In Hebrew, there are exactly twenty-six words before, and exactly twenty-six words after "Thou art with me." Is this by chance? Or was the poet boldly declaring that God being with us is the very center of our lives, the focal point of the universe? God is *with* us. We are not alone. Jesus was "Emmanuel," meaning "God *with* us." John Wesley's dying words were: "The best of all is, God is *with* us." God doesn't shelter us from trouble, God doesn't manipulate everything to suit us. But the glorious *with* is unassailable; only this fact finally matters.

There is more marvelous news in the "thou." For the first three verses of the psalm, God is spoken of in the third person: "The LORD is my shepherd . . . . He leads me . . . he restores." But with the *thou*, the third person shifts to second person: "for thou art with me . . . . Thou preparest a table . . . ." Instead of talking *about* God, the psalmist now talks *to* God; instead of God in the head, God is a friend in the heart, a conversation happens, a relationship grows.

If in the marrow of our being we believe that God is with us, then the only logical consequence would be, "I shall not want." We've read it, but have we thought about it? or lived it? "I shall not want"? Our whole life is about wanting: I look, I shop, I always want some new stuff. In our consumer culture, I shall want, I shall never stop wanting, I am instructed from childhood not merely to want, but to have.

Perhaps a better translation is "I shall lack nothing," or "I shall lack no good thing." What do I lack? Well, I lack an iPhone or a house at the coast; I lack a fully funded pension, and I lack . . . We can fill in the blank endlessly. But what do I really lack? What really matters that I do not have? What, as I grow older, would I dare not lack? The answer isn't an iPhone or vacation house. What did Jesus say to the rich young ruler (Luke 18:18–30), who claimed to be good and had plenty? "One thing you still lack." We don't lack lots of things. We lack just one: intimacy with God. The one and only thing that satisfies is God. Nothing else. No massive pile of something elses. Thou art with me; I shall lack nothing.

If "thou art with me" is the focal point of the psalm and if "I shall not want" is the beginning of new life with God, then the end is this: "I shall dwell in the house of the LORD for ever." Why do we want stuff like iPhones and vacation houses? Is it sheer coveting? I don't think so. We want communication devices because we long to connect. We want a house because — no matter how far we travel, no matter how happy or sad our nuclear family might have been—we carry inside a yearning for home. In our mobile society we may be clueless about where that might be, or if it really exists. But we still want, above all else, to go home.

If you are lucky like me, you have fond memories of summertime junkets to the home of your grandparents. For me, it was a house that I now see is rather small; but to me as a child it was large, large in love, special treats, cousins, and fun, another home, without problems or homework or chores, a special place of a more unconditional kind of love. Does God give us such places in our memory so that we will learn to desire the home for which God destines us when this life is over?

Isaac Watts's metric recasting of Psalm 23 is moving: "O may Your House be my abode. . . . There would I find a settled rest, While others go and come; No more a stranger or a guest, But like a child at home." We recoil at the idea of any child anywhere not enjoying peace and love at home—and this is evidence that God has wired into our hearts a keen sense of a proper destiny, which looks like me as a boy at my grandmother's table or on my grandfather's lap. Today we are beleaguered by urgent tasks, or we have some fun; but isn't it all a preparation for a grand homecoming, when we will "find a settled rest . . . ; no more a stranger or a guest, but like a child at home"? "Thou art with me," so "I shall not want," for "I shall dwell in the house of the LORD for ever." And it is enough.

MOr

17

1 CORINTHIANS 6:19

*Do you not know that your body is a temple of the Holy
Spirit? You are not your own; so glorify God in your body.*

L ook at your body, yourself, in the mirror. The world says
you are a consumer—that your body is to be sculpted, or
protected; it is something you use to have fun or to get ahead,
that how you look, your presentation, is everything. But if the
world dictates how I see myself, I become superficial, self-
indulgent, vapid. Thankfully, God whispers the truth about the
body, the self that I see: your body is a temple of the Holy Spirit.

Flannery O'Connor wrote a story imagining some girls in a
convent school who have just been told by an elderly, unworldly
nun that the most effective way to repel the advances of any
young man in the back seat of a car is to say, "Stop, sir! I am a
Temple of the Holy Ghost!"[1] Two of the girls jokingly began to
address each other as Temple One and Temple Two, after which
they would collapse in hysterical laughter. In our very physical,
sexually titillating culture that is obsessed with bodily comfort
and pleasure, to say, "Stop! I am a Temple of the Holy Ghost"

strikes us as comical. But what if we looked in the mirror and, instead of seeing an instrument of comfort and pleasure, we could see Temple One? And if we could look at the other person, any other person, not as another body to be evaluated by height, skin color, or usefulness, but as Temple Two?

What is a temple? A structure that exists for God, and really for no other purpose. A place of silent waiting. A place where truth is spoken, and songs are sung. A place to be deadly serious, and therefore to be giddily joyful. A place where offerings are made to God. A place where heads are bowed, where frivolous stupidity is frowned upon. A place where the unloveliest are welcomed, for the doors are open, and even if God seems to be no place else, God is there. And when you exit you wish you could linger, and you let that craving to linger manifest itself in service and holiness outside the building. A temple is a permanent ark of the covenant, bearing God's word and presence. A temple is a manger, and swaddled inside is Jesus.

So God made *me* to be all these things? Am I such a place? Isn't my life revolutionized, liberated, enlightened if I stop looking at myself as the owner of my self? Isn't the hidden secret exposed and shouted out loud when I look at my self, at my body, as owned entirely by God, and see that I exist to glorify God in my body? Do I glorify God in my body by where I take it? by what I put into it? by how I use it? by how I care for it? by what it bumps up against? or by what it refrains from bumping up against? Am I a manger, humble, nothing fancy, but mysteriously holding up Jesus for those who look closely beneath the folds of who I am?

But a temple, like any building or body, can feel empty, a bit lonely. When Paul said, "Do you not know that your body is a temple of the Holy Spirit?" he meant not merely you singular, but you *plural!* Your body, you the followers of Christ, you together are the Body of Christ, the temple of the Holy Spirit. We need each other—"where two or three are gathered" (Matt. 18:20)—to be this temple.

I love the fascinating fact that, in medieval cathedrals, many superb works of craftsmanship can be found in hidden places, where no worshiper could ever see (in the attics, behind a tower on the roof). Why? The building was intended for God, created solely for God's benefit. This is the spirit of praise. We don't do what we do to co-opt God to help us; we simply are thunderstruck by the mind and heart of God, and we worship God with our bodies; and our hidden labors, and perhaps especially those that are hidden, become a temple of the Spirit.

18

PSALM 73:1

Truly God is good to the pure in heart.

Surely God's job is to be good to us, especially if we are good. Yet the very next four words of Psalm 73 hint at a negative review of God's work: "But as for me . . . " God is good, we know we are supposed to believe — *But* as for *me* . . . The psalmist, like many of us, feels stricken; he's suffered, even though he has kept his heart generally clean; he's done the right thing — but he's had nothing but trouble and pain. If God is good, why do we suffer? Isn't God supposed to protect us?

And isn't the pain of it intensified because of the inevitable comparison to those who don't seem to be suffering? The psalmist admits that he envies the "arrogant," "the prosperity of the wicked."

> They have no pangs;
> their bodies are sound and sleek.
> They are not in trouble as other men are. . . .

Their hearts overflow with follies . . . .
All in vain have I kept my heart clean.

We are in some misery, some dissatisfaction gnaws at us, and it is worse because others seem so comfortable. A man struggles in his marriage and then looks across the restaurant at a couple who are laughing, touching hands in adoration, and his struggle is worse. A woman tries repeatedly to conceive, and then she comes to church and cascades of toddlers rampage the hallways. I can't catch up on my bills, then I overhear a guy in a Lexus eager to get to his mountain home. The comparisons pile on, and to the notion that "God is good," we mutter, "But as for me . . . "

How lovely that the Bible does not hush the "But as for me." We cry out, we teeter near the edge of giving up on God and life. But then we hear again what must be true: *Truly God is good.* God says, *Yes, I am—but what do you think is the good that I give?* We talk too loosely about God's blessings, which we think are "things," like a nice house or a good job, or even our health. But we always say these things in earshot of somebody who is chronically ill, who's lost everything. The idea that the good are rewarded and the wicked are punished is absurd to anybody paying attention. Many who are rich and healthy are not so holy; otherwise you could expect to peer in the windows of the biggest houses and find champions of morality and piety. Don't we all know people who are extraordinarily good and holy but who suffer awfully?

Tempted to give up on God, the psalmist goes into the sanctuary (v. 17) and then truth dawns. He discovers there that God *is* good. But the "good" God gives isn't this or that tangible reward; the "good" isn't health or wealth. What God gives is God's own self. Listen to the transparent passion and simple eloquence of the psalmist:

There is nothing upon earth that I desire besides thee.
My flesh and my heart may fail,
but God is the strength of my heart and my portion for ever. . . .
For me it is good to be near God.

As you grow older, you do not care much what you get from your family for Christmas or your birthday, but you care immensely whether they show up or not. God shows up, God's presence is good. "For me it is good to be near God."

Who is this God? Not the great cashier in the sky who rewards our goodness, and not the weaver of an invisible spell of protection around us. God is love, God is the one who came down and suffered a terrible death while his friends ran for shelter. God looks down on our suffering and does not say, "It is my will." Instead, God bears our suffering, engaging in stunning solidarity with us in our "But as for me . . . "

God is near, whether we feel it or not, because God promised. Jesus trusted that promise when the devil tried to get his claws into him, when his friends abandoned him, when he cried out, "My God, why have you forsaken me?" We trust the undeniable fact of God's presence, not our feelings about God's presence or apparent lack thereof.

God's good is God's own self; and if so, a "pure heart" must not mean merely doing nice things or avoiding what's naughty. The heart's best is love. The pure in heart love. We love God now, and the greatest conceivable gift is that our love relationship with God continues, it cannot be severed: this is eternal life.

The psalmist learned it was "good to be near God" only when he came to the sanctuary and to "the congregation." The Church, the body of believers, is near. They know how to love, to offer prayers and bake casseroles, profound manifestations of God's presence. Invisibly but surely, that great hovering communion of the saints still lurks in every sanctuary, martyrs, believers, grandparents, teachers, and holy friends who may seem dead and gone but are no more dead and gone than the God we need so desperately. One moment we feel alone and desolate; but in the sanctuary we are enveloped in much love, God's love, the Church's love, and we nod, recognizing the only good that matters—and it is enough: As for me, "it is good to be near God."

19

MATTHEW 7:12

*Whatever you wish that [others] would do to you, do so
to them.*

How odd is it that Jesus' most famous saying (the so-called
Golden Rule — "Do unto others as you would have them
do unto you") is seemingly out of character for him? and not
really translated correctly? Perhaps we latch onto Jesus' words,
foolishly thinking he's advocating tit for tat, the greasing of
palms: cut a business partner in on a deal, and he'll help you
make some dough next time; whisper a rumor and hope something gets whispered back; rub my back, I'll rub yours; we're
wheelin' and dealin' with Jesus' endorsement.

But wasn't Jesus the one who said, "Turn the other cheek"
(Matt. 5:39)? "Invite those to dinner who cannot invite you
back" (Luke 14:13–14)? "Love your enemies" (Matt. 5:44)?
"Lend, expecting nothing in return" (Luke 6:35)? Why would
Jesus suddenly play "even Steven" with "Do unto others"?

Notice Jesus did *not* say, "Do unto others *so* they will do
unto you," or, "Do unto others *before* they do unto you," or, "Do
unto others as they *have done* to you." Notice Jesus actually

didn't even say, "Do unto others as you would have them do unto you." Instead of starting with you as the one acting, Jesus begins with how you feel about being treated by someone else's action: "Whatever you wish [others] would do to you, do so to them." See the difference? Jesus was speaking to people who were disregarded as nobodies, who never got any respect, who had nothing. Jesus invited the mistreated, who only fantasized about receiving a little respect and kindness, to imagine how they wish they could be treated—and then to act that way toward others.

When Jesus suggested "Whatever you wish others would do to you, do so to them," he was in the thick of a stunning conversation about asking and gift giving—and especially the way God gives far more generously than we do. The world teaches us to focus on our selves: it's all about me: What am I getting out of this, what's in it for me? Like Narcissus, we gaze into the mirror and think we see in our own reflection the center of the universe.

Sometimes even our charitable acts, those times we volunteer in mission, are more about us than others. I deliver meals to shut-ins "to feel good about myself"; I tutor to have something shiny on my college application; I cut a check to the church to get a tax deduction. But Jesus invites us into a life that isn't about me—my life is about others. What should I do for them, with them? Not what makes me feel good, but in my imagination I try to get inside their heads. I remember times I felt left out, in need, lonely, desolate, lost. What might have helped? Then I act, not to gain anything for myself, except the sheer joy of being in sync with our Lord's wisdom.

And speaking of our Lord: we can always reflect upon Jesus, who must have taken "Whatever you wish that [others] would do to you, do so to them" very seriously for himself. What did Jesus do to other people? That must be what Jesus wishes we would do. Jesus loved. Jesus touched the untouchables. Jesus respectfully asked questions and conversed on the things of God. Jesus was tender, compassionate—and in his pattern of action we discover our blueprint for living. What he did to others must be what he wishes we would do too.

Sometimes we watch the evening news and wish the world were different. Perhaps our city is weighted down with so many problems. The neighborhood isn't what it used to be. Attending church can be frustrating since nobody signs up for anything, and the hypocrites appear to have taken over. My own family is a mess. I wish somebody would do something. To us, Jesus says, "Whatever you wish others would do to you, do so to them," and that includes "Whatever you wish others would do, do it yourself." Grab a hand and get somebody to join you; but even if nobody will come just now, go anyway. You won't really be alone, because Jesus said, "Whatever you wish others would do to you, do so to them," and he never neglects his own words, so he will be with you until (and even after) others catch on and come with you.

Mar
8

20

JEREMIAH 29:11

I know the plans I have for you, says the LORD, plans for good and not for evil, to give you a future and a hope. (au. trans.)

When I was working on my book *The Will of God*, I conversed with many people about questions like "Why do bad things happen?" and "What does God want me to do?" Frequently friends would ask, "How can I know God's plan for my life?" I thumbed through books from wise authors, and I rifled through the Scriptures to gather up a few clues—and came up with nothing much at all.

Does God have "a plan for my life"? As appealing as this may be, and as caring and personal as God always is, the fact is the Bible just doesn't say a word about God having a blueprint, a script, a "plan" for my life, for how I will grow up, whom I will marry, how things will unfold, even when I will die. In a way, such a "plan" might be comforting; but then, do we really want to be pawns on God's chessboard, being moved about with no responsibility? What about when someone does something horrible? Is God planning to lace your life with misery now and then?

Don't we embrace the wish for "God's plan for my life" because we are fearful? We do not like to think of life unfolding haphazardly. We like to think God has earthly happiness mapped out for us. But what if God is actually calling us to suffer for Christ? What if what God yearns for from us is sacrifice? God says, "Follow me," and we go, not knowing where we might be led—and that is the beauty of following, with no awareness of any plan. God woos us, shapes us, and join hands in an adventure that will wind up who knows where, but the journey is all good since we are near God.

If we read Jeremiah 29:11 carefully, we notice that God's "plans for good" are not for Jeremiah, or for any other individual. The word "you" (in "the plans I have for you") is plural; in the South, God would say "the plans I have for y'all." The future, the hope God gives "you" ("y'all") is for a crowd, for the community, for the nation. God called Jeremiah to speak God's Word, not to this man or woman, or just to you or me, but to the nation of Israel during its most perilous time in history.

Israel is not our nation, and Israel isn't just any random nation. Israel is the nation God chose because God wanted to use Israel to save the world. When it appeared Israel was crumbling and probably would cease to exist, God declared that God wasn't through with Israel yet; God's promises to use Israel were not broken.

So who is the "y'all" God has plans for now? Israel? Perhaps. The United States? America just isn't on the Old Testament radar screen. Could it be the Church? Aren't we the "y'all" God promises to use for good? God is not through with the Church, the coalesced body of believers who, by the grace of God, never lose their destined role for the sake of the world. God has plans for the Church; Church is about being God's instrument—not whether it suits me or entertains me. I never go solo with God; my life in God's plan is interwoven with others in God's "y'all." I do not, therefore, lose my individuality, but I finally discover it when I find my proper place in the Body of Christ.

How good of God, not to make us go it alone, but to give us good company in the life of faith! I would clarify that this doesn't make God's plan less personal, but *more* personal. If you are part of a family, or a team, it isn't less personal that you are one among others; there is more love, meaningful sharing—you don't have to bear life alone. Part of God's plan is that "It is not good for you to be alone" (Gen. 2:18); God gives us fellowship, the dizzying privilege of being part of something bigger than just me or my life.

To our Bible students, we plead and cajole: "Context, context, context!" Browse through all of Jeremiah, and then read all of chapter 29 closely. Nebuchadnezzar's Babylonian juggernaut has conquered Jerusalem, reducing the city to rubble, marching the few survivors off to live hundreds of miles away in exile. Through the prophet Jeremiah, God advises the people to settle down, to take the long-term view; God will not sweep down in the next seventy minutes to rescue the people. They have, not seventy minutes or seventy days, but seventy years to wait before God acts decisively to redeem the people of Israel.

Seventy years? Who will be around then? Only the youngest children had a chance to live so long. So God's plan cannot be thwarted, but God's plan also isn't instantaneous; stellar patience, a dogged hope, a willingness to cope with unrealized dreams is required of us—and a profound trust in God's good purpose. "Nothing that is worth doing can be achieved in our lifetime; therefore we must be saved by hope" (Reinhold Niebuhr).[1]

21

1 SAMUEL 16:7

The LORD sees not as man sees; man looks on the outward appearance, but the LORD looks on the heart.

What is the Bible? Not a Ouija board or an answer book, but some amazingly effective eyeglasses that can correct our shortsightedness, our blurred vision.

Consider this story out of the Bronze Age: God informs Samuel that one of Jesse's sons will be the next king of Israel. Sizing up the young men, Samuel is impressed by the big boys, the swashbuckling Eliab, the muscular Abinadab. Surely one of these will be God's chosen leader. But one by one God says no. In the end, it is David, the one Jesse had not even thought to include among the candidates, who is the one the Lord will use! The Bible's logic trumps in once more: it is the smallest, the weakest, the unlikely one that God uses, the one who relies not on his own strength, but has a "heart" for God, the one who is available to God, dependent upon God.

Faith is a new way of seeing, as if by X-ray, not fooled by the surface of things, but looking deeper, never gawking over the superficialities the world panders to, but sensitive only to love, caring about what is of eternal significance. But faith isn't a squinting, a straining of the eye; we come to see the way God sees the same way we come to recognize the words of a foreign language on a page: through sitting in class, flipping back and forth through a textbook, a dictionary, getting the hang of the grammar, practicing, making laughable mistakes, trying again. After all, the Bible was written in an alien language; its words have strange meanings. Up is really down, and great is nothing; the simple is complex, and the lowly is absolutely marvelous.

Foolishness is the rage, and the meek, poor, and grieving are counted as blessed. Tolkien's wise wizard Gandalf understood how to see: "All that is gold does not glitter . . . ."[1] This is our prayer: "O Lord, help me learn to *see* the way you see when I look at anybody—the stranger, coworker, sibling, friend, spouse."

In the comedy film *Bruce Almighty*, the insensitive, knuckle-headed Bruce is finally broken down by life, having squandered his relationship with Grace. God asks him, "What do you really want, Bruce? Do you want Grace back?" Bruce, finally understanding, surprises even God by saying, "No. I want her to meet somebody who will love her, who will see her the way I see her now—through your eyes."

To see as the Lord sees may cause us a few tears. When Jesus looked over the holy city of Jerusalem, he wept; when he saw his friend Lazarus had died, Jesus wept. When we see the world the way the Lord sees it, we will inevitably grieve with the divine heartbreak. And sharing God's tears might help us to see: apart from God's tears we might look past the ache the next person harbors, we might flit off to a party and forget children are hungry or war is raging. But when we see as the Lord sees, we notice—and we might even *do* something. We become visionaries, and we do not merely look, but we go, we act, we become the eyes and hands of Christ.

Going farther: do I dare to be *seen* the way the Lord sees? The Lord looks on my heart. This notion frightens me at first, for I know my heart is a tangle of darkness, mixed motives, a tug-of-war between noble impulses and tawdry cravings. But the Lord keeps looking, the Lord is merciful, the Lord never stops seeking an opening, a vulnerable willingness in my heart that says, "This is who I am, make me into who you are." The facade crashes down, and I discover the love and empowering direction of God. Then I'm not impressed by or daunted by what plunged me into fear yesterday. I see myself, and you, and the stranger, the way the Lord sees. I even begin to see God clearly, perhaps for the first time.

And to understand what God asks. I have generally thought that Jesse brought out his big boys and left David out in the field because he assumed they were the strong, strapping, likely candidates, and David was just too small. But I wonder. Perhaps Jesse had a special affection for David; perhaps he sensed David, though young, was the most wonderfully gifted one — and so Jesse wanted to protect him, to hide him away in the field, lest he be put in harm's way. When we see as the Lord sees, we acknowledge the risk, but we remember that God foresaw the risk but did not hold back his beloved son, Jesus, and our newfound vision prevents us from holding back what God asks of us, no matter how scary it seems.

I need the corrective lenses, and a heavy dose of God's focusing power. So I'll pray the words conceived by Richard of Chichester nearly eight hundred years ago, made popular in that great song from *Godspell*: "Oh dear Lord, three things I pray—to see thee more clearly, love thee more dearly, follow thee more nearly day by day."

22

PSALM 1:1–2

*Blessed is the man who walks not in the counsel of the
wicked, nor stands in the way of sinners, nor sits in the
seat of scoffers; but his delight is in the law of the LORD,
and on his law he meditates day and night.*

How fascinating: the book of Psalms, the prayer book of the
Bible, Israel's hymnal, opens with a poem about ethics!
Prayer and worship are ultimately about a changed life; God
wants to pervade the part of you that chooses, in a thousand
little decisions and the occasional big Decision. Do you "walk in
the counsel of the wicked"? or "delight in the law of the LORD"?

Framed this way, it's no choice at all, is it? Who would know-
ingly choose destruction? Will I jump off a cliff? or sit down to
a sumptuous dinner with those I love? Will I ruin my life? or
fulfill my destiny? But if the choice is so easy, why then do we
find our ears perking up to the whispering of wickedness?

The "counsel of the wicked" is sneaky, isn't it? The devil
doesn't jump out in a red suit, wielding a blazing pitchfork; no,
the devil dresses up like an angel of light, promising you the
moon. The "good life" as defined by society fools us; this life of
wealth, pleasure, leisure is vapid, and leaves you hollow inside.
God's adventure is the richness of generosity and prayer, the

pleasure of service and worship, the leisure of Sabbath rest and silence in the presence of God. Society says "Don't break the law, maximize your portfolio, get ahead"—but the Psalm shakes its head and pities us for missing the "delight . . . in the law of the LORD."

Robert Frost wrote, "Two roads diverged in a yellow wood, And sorry I could not travel both . . . " But we think we *can* travel both—or more than two. I'm in a clearing, four roads diverge, and I can't miss a thing: I'll take all four! But we cannot take four, or seven, or even two; you wind up splintered, divided, out of focus, and the road "less traveled," the delight in the law of the Lord, seems boring or restrictive, when in fact it is the true joy of every heart.

Some scholars like to translate "Blessed" as "Happy," although we had better be careful. Our frenetic quest for "happiness" can deflect us from God. Clint McCann explained Psalm 1 well: "Happiness involves not enjoying oneself but delight in the teaching of God. The goal of life is to be found not in self-fulfillment but in praising God. Prosperity does not involve getting what one wants; rather, it comes from being connected to the source of life."[1] How do we shift from the chase for self-fulfillment and connect to the source of life?

Psalm 1 speaks of meditating on God's law "day and night." You can't stay up all night reading the Bible; you have to earn a living, eat, clean house, and exercise. But is there a way to make "the law of the LORD" a streaming, omnipresent reality in our daily routine? We begin by making a devotional regimen as essential as brushing our teeth, we plant little mnemonic devices (a cross, a printed prayer, a picture of St. Francis) in the desk, bathroom, kitchen, car. But can we begin to conceive of God as a constant companion?

Sometimes when I travel I am alone, and it's not as much fun as when I travel with my wife, my children, or a friend. The joy of walking together, pointing ("Did you see that?"), sharing a meal, chatting over the highlights and challenges of the day: can we imagine what isn't imaginary at all—that we are never alone, that God is there beside us wherever we find ourselves? I talk to myself more than I care to admit. Can I talk instead to God? Do I behave differently if God is there? Isn't the comfort of God's lingering presence the holy solution to the nagging loneliness we bear deep inside?

Can what I read in the Bible last night come alive in a seemingly unreligious situation today? Some people love Bible study, but to others it feels corny, irrelevant, abstruse somehow. But Jesus called "disciples" (a word meaning "students"). God wants to be known, understood, reflected upon, explored intellectually: we are wired to discover immense fulfillment in the simple probing of the heart and nature of God, in the mental stimulation of reliving the Bible's stories and singing its songs.

Americans cherish the "pursuit of happiness." But notice what the historian David McCullough said about the Founding Fathers:

> To them, the "pursuit of happiness" . . . meant the life of the mind and spirit. It meant education and the love of learning. John Adams, in a letter to his son John Quincy when the boy was a student at the University of Leiden, stressed that he should carry a book with him wherever he went. It was his happiness that mattered, Adams told him. "You will never be alone with a poet in your pocket."[2]

The psalmist is the poet you keep in your pocket; with God's Word you will never be alone.

23

GALATIANS 5:1

*For freedom Christ has set us free; stand fast therefore,
and do not submit again to a yoke of slavery.*

Freedom: Americans celebrate July 4 with picnics, fireworks, and fun. Freedom (the way John Locke and the Founding Fathers who read him so diligently would have conceived it): A native property of the soul, and we are to be vigilant to shield that inborn drive to self-determination from governments or anybody out there. Freedom: Our highest ideal, it is never to be infringed upon or limited.

How interesting is it, then, that in the history of Christianity one of the most ferocious debates has been over whether we are free or not. St. Augustine argued with Pelagius and won, as did Martin Luther with Erasmus: you may feel free, but you are not free at all. Rifling through the pages of Scripture and thinking deeply about their own lives, they realized that freedom is not something you indelibly have; it is not at all an unalienable right. Your will, the part of you that decides, feels, and acts, is shackled. We are creatures of habit, driven by compulsions, hooked on sin; we are addicts, if you will. Like Paul, we discover that "I do not do the good I want" (Rom. 7:19). Peer deeply into your soul and you notice a kind of combat being waged; you cannot simply "just say no." And isn't it obvious that the most important facts of your life (your parents, race, gender, place of birth) are entirely unchosen?

Freedom, the way we have been tutored to cherish it, is a kind of enslavement. Freedom trumps reason, as my unconstrained will must do as it wishes, no matter how irrational the desire. Freedom trumps love, as my ever supreme will chooses always for me, and you'd better give me my space. Freedom is its own justification and can validate almost anything, from commitment-breaking to war.

Freedom can become slavery to impulse, and we are dehumanized. Natan Sharansky, the former Soviet dissident, wrote of his time in a gulag:

> In freedom, I am lost in a myriad of choices. When I walk on the street, dozens of cheeses, fruits, and juices stare at me from store windows. An endless series of decisions . . . must be made: What to drink in the morning? What to do in the evening? Which friends to visit? In the punishment cell, life was much simpler. Every day brought only one choice: good or evil, white or black, saying yes or no to the KGB. Moreover, I had all the time I needed to think about these choices, to concentrate on the most fundamental problems of existence, to test myself in fear, in hope, in belief, in love. And now, lost in thousands of mundane choices, I suddenly realize that there's no time to reflect on the bigger questions. How to enjoy the vivid colors of freedom without losing the existential depth I felt in prison?[1]

Is freedom a jammed shopping basket? What about existential depth, saying yes or no on the big questions?

For Paul, freedom isn't something you have; it is precisely what you do *not* have until you are "set free" by the Spirit. Freedom—theologically speaking—is more akin to surrender, applying the brakes to my doing as I wish, opening myself to the power of God. As Frederick Buechner put it, "We have freedom to the degree that the master whom we obey grants it to us in return for our obedience."[2]

Freedom — Christianity-style — is the joyful liberation of the one who has shed any notion of "I will do as I wish," happily assuming the prayerful posture of "Lord, not my will, but your will be done." Freedom is the thank-you note you write to God the great Physician for healing your diseased soul. Freedom is freedom from sin, freedom from hollowness, from pointlessness, from our proclivity to wound each other, from sorrow. The Spirit sets us free to love, to trust, to serve, to experience the beauty of life with God.

Freedom is Jesus. We may think that freedom looks like a flag rippling in the breeze, or a soldier standing at attention, or that Trumbull painting of the signing of the Declaration of Independence, or perhaps even an empty calendar, a shopping mall, a wad of cash in your pocket with which you can do whatever you please. But if you want to see real freedom, look to Jesus, the only person who was truly free. He freely came down the ladder of power into a humble manger; he freely left his livelihood to follow God; he freely courted violence against himself out of his love for total strangers; he freely exhibited God's free grace when the soldiers handcuffed him; he freely refused to wield his immense power as he breathed his last; he freely forgave, freely rose, freely rules in humble love, and freely sets us prisoners free.

24

PSALM 98:5–6

Sing praises to the LORD with the lyre and the sound of melody! With trumpets make a joyful noise before the King, the LORD!

Once in a while I try in my mind to imagine the sound of these ancient musical instruments, and the faces and hearts of the Israelites who played them. When they thought of God, their first reflex was *praise*. Our first reflex might be far more utilitarian: I ask God for stuff, I measure God by whether God seems to be doing what I need, or I question God.

But Israel praised. Praise is our amazement at God, our recognition of the power and tenderness of the Creator. Praise enjoys and celebrates God's love; praise is our best attempt to feel, say, or sing something appropriate to God. Praise doesn't ask, "What have you done for me lately?" but instead exclaims, "How great Thou art!" Walter Brueggemann explains: "All of life exists for the sake of God. Praise articulates and embodies our capacity to yield, submit, and abandon ourselves in trust and gratitude to the One whose we are. God is addressed not because we have need, but simply because God is God."[1]

Praise doesn't "work," it is not productive, it isn't about me. Praise is downright wasteful in terms of possible ways to spend your time. To think of God like a lover, one on whom you might dote for hours, requires considerable imagination, a radical reshaping of the soul.

When St. Augustine insightfully probed the love of God, he wrote in Latin, a language featuring a pair of distinct words we might translate as "love": *uti* and *frui*.[2] There is *uti* love, love of "use": I love money because I can use it to get something else I really want. But then there is *frui* love, love of "enjoyment": I love chocolate because . . . well, I just love chocolate, apart from what I get out of it. God wants to be loved with *frui* love, although more often than not we come at God with *uti* love, hoping to co-opt God to help us with our pet projects. Praise strives for *frui*, the love of enjoyment, so we might glorify God and enjoy God forever.

A few years ago I spoke at a conference of Pentecostal clergy. During the opening hymn (which lasted at least twenty minutes), the man sitting next to me drifted away from what everyone else was singing and simply lifted his hands toward the ceiling (or heaven) and muttered, over and over, "Oh Jesus, you are so beautiful. Oh Jesus, you are so beautiful." He wasn't saying, "Oh Jesus, could you do me a favor?"

Israel praised with makeshift instruments which craftsmen labored over—and their sole purpose was to produce sound that would rise to the skies and be heard by God. Psalm 98 speaks of the lyre. Wasn't the lyre the instrument Orpheus played in that mythological story? Sailors, seduced by the songs of the sirens, couldn't avoid shipwreck. Odysseus managed to sail past their perilous rocks by stuffing wax in the ears of the rowers and strapping himself to the mast of the ship; but Orpheus simply pulled out his lyre and played a song more beautiful than that of the sirens, and the rowers listened to his song and sailed to safety.

Praise is our best counter to evil in the world. If we are "lost in wonder, love, and praise," there is not much chance we will be seduced into tawdry sin or find ourselves jaded and cynical. Praise is the cure for despair and loneliness; if we "make a joyful noise to the LORD," we experience a quiet in the soul, a community of love.

Psalm 98 praises the Lord "for he has done marvelous things! . . . [He] has made known his victory" (vv. 1–2). Weaving the universe into existence, fashioning the delicate petals on a rose or crafting massive canyons, musing in wisdom, promising eternal bliss: the greatness of God could occupy us for every minute of every day as we notice some new aspect of the divine wonder. We would never grow weary or exhaust the possibilities. Of course, the most marvelous "thing" God ever did was to visit us on earth. Jesus, by simply showing up, by teaching, touching, suffering, and rising, was and is marvelous, and so beautiful as to make you blush. Jesus is the victory of God—and our only sensible response is not to co-opt him into aiding us with our agenda, but simply to praise.

Late in her life, Dorothy Day was asked to write an autobiography. She thought awhile and then said she couldn't, because she kept thinking about Jesus and his visit long ago, his love, his grace, and how fortunate she had been "to have had Jesus on my mind for so long."[3] It's the beautiful song; we hear it and we are safe, we are delighted, we are home.

25

⟳

PSALM 130:4

There is forgiveness with thee, that thou mayest be feared.

How strange! Psalm 130:4 seems to suggest that the purpose of forgiveness is that God might be feared. But isn't faith supposed to obliterate fear? Isn't the purpose of forgiveness that—well, that I can be forgiven?

Perhaps the theologians from centuries ago were right: religion isn't about me getting my spiritual life in order or about me ensuring my eternal destiny. Maybe it's about God, the glory of God—and when we focus on the wonder of God, the magnificence of God, and our jaws drop in awestruck wonder, then we have discovered our reason for existence.

Why would the psalm hope to instill fear? We may say that the "fear" of God is more like reverence, and it is. Perhaps also there is a proper kind of fear, not fearing this or that circumstance in life, but trembling in dead earnest before the God whose immense power translates into tender love. The old hymn sings, "'Twas grace that taught my heart to fear." And think about Exodus 20:20: "Do not fear; for God has come to prove you, and that the fear of him may be before your eyes, that you may not sin."

The lessons hidden in Psalm 130:4 and Exodus 20:20 are many. Don't we suffer from a shallow, flabby understanding of mercy and forgiveness? Aren't we both permissive, and yet unable to show much mercy? Could it be that we will have to relearn mercy before we can ratchet up our moral standards? Mercy implies a demanding morality, doesn't it?

We are terribly confused about forgiveness; we foolishly think forgiveness means "Oh, it doesn't matter." But forgiveness is when we say, "This matters so much we've got to do something about it. We've got to reconcile." Reconciliation isn't easy. Forgiveness is the hardest work, yet the larger fear is not to reconcile. You have to dig stuff up and wrestle with it. You must be brutally honest, yet kind. You listen deeply enough to understand those hidden causes of what has gone on between you and the other person. Forgiveness isn't always a warm, fuzzy feeling. If you forgive me, it doesn't mean you feel like showering me with hugs and kisses. Forgiveness is a decision, a commitment to look at me through God's eyes, to stick with me.

Forgiveness is business with God, although we frequently fret more about the idea that somebody out there might be out of sorts with us. Yes, we care about reconciliation with others; but the primal relationship to consider is ours with God; forgiveness is with God, and we had best find it there first, and then forgiveness among our fellows will become lively.

God forgives. God looks at us through God's eyes; God sticks with us. Shakespeare spoke of mercy as "twice blest; It blesseth him that gives and him that takes: . . . Though justice be thy plea, consider this, that, in the course of justice, none of us should see salvation."[1] But could it be that mercy and justice are not opposites, but rather friends, two elements that, if combined in the laboratory of life with God, work some healing alchemy in the soul? We are forgiven so God might be feared; we receive mercy so we might be holy. Fear God! Then do not fear, for God has come to prove you, that you may not sin. It's the power of mercy.

Any mercy worth its salt has healing power hidden within. It would never be enough simply to be merciful—in the sense of letting bygones be bygones, of continuing to love despite whatever has transpired. God is better than that: God does not rest until the one forgiven is the one transformed. God's power not only sustains a relationship but simultaneously raises the bar, and the behavior, for those in the relationship.

The Book of Common Prayer invites us to say to God each day, "Imprint upon our hearts such a dread of thy judgments, and such a grateful sense of thy goodness to us, as may make us both afraid and ashamed to offend thee." If we look to the cross, if we weigh in our hearts the startling suffering, and thus love, of Christ for us, for me, then we come to a kind of fear, the kind a parent feels in the presence of a newborn child, the kind you sense if you consider a soldier losing life and limb in a foreign war, or a child patting the brow of a parent dying over many days, or what it feels like to climb a towering mountain only to discover even more heights beyond the crest, and when we draw very close to the heart of God, and we are grasped by the wisdom the world counts as folly: "There is forgiveness with thee, that thou mayest be feared."

26

MATTHEW 5:9

*Blessed are the peacemakers, for they shall be called
sons of God.*

The angels sang "Peace on earth" at Jesus' birth. When he
grew up, Jesus said, "Blessed are the peacemakers." The
Greek word literally means "doers of peace" or "makers of
peace." *Paci-fist* means "peace-maker."

Some think of "pacifism" as "passivism," as if "peace" suggests we do nothing or that we be passive in the face of evil. But
Jesus did not say, "Blessed are those who are passive and do
nothing," but "Blessed are the doers, the makers of peace." To
do peace, to make peace, you have to get busy, you have to act;
you have a world of work ahead of you.

Think about your family, your coworkers, anybody, everybody. There is tension, even warfare, but Christians never shrug
their shoulders; they doggedly make peace. Christians never
settle for the bogus kind of peace that pretends, politely nurses
old grievances, or privately harbors piercing criticisms. We seek
out the other person and strive valiantly for peace. Christians
never settle for peace by mere force. If Dad shouts and waves a

mighty fist, and his wife and children cower silently, there is no peace in that home.

Genuine peace is deeper, richer, giving life to those in the home, and in the world, not walking on eggshells but dancing in the streets, clenched fists opening, receiving the once-clenched fist of another, a veritable Virginia reel of joy. Peace, when we labor to make peace, opens a faucet that lets a poison run out of the soul, and in the emptied place deep joy flows.

Dietrich Bonhoeffer said, "There can only be peace when it does not rest on lies and injustice."[1] Christians dare to speak the truth with the one from whom we are alienated—gently, tenderly, and listening, expecting the other person has some truth to tell too. We learn how to disagree, not how to avoid discomfort.

For peace to be made, some shift in power must happen. For a tall, muscular guy with a big sword to be at peace with a little unarmed, scrawny guy, the big guy has to relinquish his bigness; he has to decide not to tower in intimidation, and the little guy has to decide not to run, not to be a sneaky guerilla. When the strong befriend the weak, dignity and strength are imparted to the weak—although the dignity and strength flow both ways, don't they?

Peacemaking is all about love, which isn't a mood: love acts. Jesus said, "Love your enemies." Love really is "the only force capable of transforming an enemy into a friend. We never get rid of an enemy by meeting hate with hate; we get rid of an enemy by getting rid of enmity. By its very nature, hate destroys and tears down; by its very nature, love creates and builds up" (Martin Luther King).[2]

Wasn't Bonhoeffer right? "The forgiveness of sins still remains the sole ground of all peace."[3] We may "kiss and make up" or paste on pretended peace, when our real need is to dive into the thicket of the issue and try to understand, acknowledge, strategize, and forgive. We may shrink back from forgiveness, from peacemaking, not merely because it's hard work, but because there can be something darkly delicious about an unhealed grievance. Unforgiven sin tangles us up in some barbed wire that lacerates the soul.

Peacemakers are heroes. St. Francis went on crusade with armed warriors, but walked unarmed across no-man's-land to the Muslim warriors who were about to kill him—but he was a laughingstock, so they took him to the sultan, who listened to Francis talk about his faith and nearly converted.[4] Francis made peace—as he did with a wolf who had terrorized the citizens of Gubbio. Francis went into the hills, and the wolf ran out snarling. Francis urged the wolf to repent of this great evil; but he told the wolf he understood why the wolf had devoured people: there was no food in those hills. So he struck a deal: What if the people feed you? Will you stop eating them? The wolf lifted his paw, and Francis led the wolf into the village. The people were uneasy at first, but came to love the wolf, treating him like a pet. They mourned when he died two years later.

What greater need could we have in our world than the making of peace—in the world, in our communities, our homes, our hearts? How could we possibly get closer to Christ, who was and is himself "our peace, who has made us both one, and has broken down the dividing wall of hostility" (Eph. 2:14)?

27

PROVERBS 16:7

When a man's ways please the LORD, he makes even his enemies to be at peace with him.

Even his enemies! It pleases the Lord when we make peace, not just with peaceable people like us, but even with our enemies. Or perhaps the proverb reaches deeper: when someone's ways please the Lord, then . . . then? Once we realize our ways please the Lord? Or once we seek God's good favor? Then we make even our enemies to be at peace with us?

Some self-righteous folks think that a raging conflict is a sign that I am in sync with God. If I have the right answers about God or morality, if I am on a crusade for goodness, then I expect recrimination, and I even have every right to be ugly and intimidating in manner, so holy is my cause! But God is peace, and when we live in ways that are pleasing to God, "even [our] enemies" are at peace with us. Can this be? Isn't it the enemy's fault for being an enemy?

We please God by our humility, by exhibiting an expansive mind full of wisdom, by a prayerfulness that enlarges the heart. Dietrich Bonhoeffer suggested that peace requires truth-fulness and forgiveness—the dispositions God treasures most highly, the miracles God works in those close to him. The one who pleases the Lord takes responsibility for the enmity of the enemy, owns it, offers it to God, and strives for reconciliation.[1]

Jesus said "Blessed are the peacemakers" and "Love your enemies" (Matt. 5:9, 44). The wise never settle for seemingly inevitable conflicts with people. They recall Martin Luther King's insight that love transforms enemies into friends.

And notice the proverb says "makes even his enemies to be at peace." You can't force them, can you? But perhaps we can; perhaps we labor diligently, peacefully, but tirelessly, to befriend the foe. Jesus said, "Blessed are the peacemakers," those who make peace happen, not by force or manipulation, but by love, humility, a spacious openness that refuses to settle for anything less than peace—for peace is pleasing to the Lord.

We love the idea of love, the notion of peace—but as Jesus asked, "If you love those who love you, what reward have you? Do not even the tax collectors do the same?" (Matt. 5:46). What good is it to love those who love you? What about those who are hard to love, who make peace difficult, who think wrong, who offend our sensibilities? The proverb gently and alluringly suggests that it is precisely these who offer us the possibility of pleasing the Lord.

Jesus not only taught peace. His life (and death) mission was to make even his enemies to be at peace with him. He befriended the unloved, touched the untouchables, forgave the soldiers in his own crucifixion detail, had a kind of mercy on Pilate, and died so that we who, by sin or just plain malaise and a slack atti-tude, have made ourselves enemies of God might be the recipi-ents of grace and might be joined to the Jesus with whom God the Father was "well pleased."

Think how pleased God was the day Francis of Assisi arrived in Monte Casale. One of the friars said that, just a few min-utes earlier, they had run off some bad men, would-be thieves. Francis said, "I must pursue them!" So he walked swiftly down the road until he caught up with them—and surprised them by giving them some bread and wine, assuming they were hungry. Then he invited them to be hungry no longer: "Come and live with us in the house at Monte Casale." And so they did—and became friars in the order of St. Francis.

God's dream of peace is a word of mercy. St. Augustine imagined that, if you would pierce your neighbor with a sword of anger, that sword first passes through your own heart and wounds you more brutally. Jesus was wounded for our peace, to put an end to our wounding each other and ourselves. Then, and not until then, God will be pleased, confirming the lovely truth that "when a man's ways please the LORD, he makes even his enemies to be at peace with him."

28

2 CORINTHIANS 9:7

For God loves a cheerful giver.

Like most fund-raisers, Paul eloquently tries to persuade the Christians in ancient Corinth to part with their money so he can corral enough shekels to stave off the desperate needs of the poor. We wonder if he met his goal.

"God loves a cheerful giver." Paul does not say, "God loves a grudging giver, God loves a guilty giver, God loves a calculating giver, God loves the giver who tosses in some spare change." And Paul does not say, "God doesn't love an uncheerful giver, God is enraged with a nongiver, God blushes when he sees the chintzy giver."

What is Paul up to? God loves everybody, of course—but perhaps you never get the love, you don't let it into your self, if you are forever guarding and measuring what you dole out. God's love frees you to give "cheerfully." The Greek for "cheerful" is *hilaron*, as in "hilarious." Sometimes our giving is "hilarious," pathetically small, given what God has done for us. But our giving can become "hilarious," as in being caught off guard by the delight, the sheer joy, and even the hilarity the gift brings to the one in need.

St. Francis of Assisi turned charitable giving into raucous hilarity, and others were infected by the contagion of joy—none more so than Brother Juniper, who exhibited the giddy mirth of a holy life. His love for the poor was so great that if he saw someone in need, he would give away the very clothes off his back. Finally his guardian ordered him not to give his tunic, or any part of it, to a beggar.

But soon Juniper was approached by a pauper asking for alms. He replied, "I have nothing to give, except this tunic, and I cannot give it to you due to my vow of obedience. However, if you steal it from me, I will not stop you." Left naked, Juniper returned to the other friars and told them he had been robbed. His compassion became so great that he gave away, not only his own things, but the books, altar linens, and capes belonging to other friars. When the poor came to Brother Juniper, the other friars would hide their belongings so he could not find them.[1] No wonder people thought of him as an angel—no doubt in the sense Chesterton imagined when he suggested that angels can fly because they take themselves so lightly. Cheerful givers travel more lightly than the rest of us.

Today the Church is in the peculiar business of cajoling its members every year to give, to meet the budget, to respond to new needs that have emerged. Paul has needs in mind, but he is not much interested in the worthiness of the recipients of the giving. Paul is gravely concerned for the salvation of the givers. The motivation to give isn't the need, it's the blessing. In the previous verse, Paul spoke of those who sow "bountifully." This doesn't just mean they give a lot. The Greek translated "bountifully" is *ep eulogiais*, meaning "from blessing" or "with thanksgiving." We give because we have been blessed; we give to demonstrate our profound gratitude to God. Jesus said, "Freely you have received; freely give" (Matt. 10:8). How generous has God been, with sunshine, the breath you just took, the miracle of vision and thought, the symphony of nature, people who have put up with you, and most splendidly the love of Jesus, who was not stingy or calculating, but gave up his very life for me and for you?

Things have value, but we subvert their true value by clinging to them, in the same way we ruin relationships with people if we grasp after them instead of letting them bloom freely. Whenever St. Francis was given a gift, he would always ask the giver for permission to give it away if he should meet someone in need. In Marilynne Robinson's novel *Gilead*, the narrator says, "My grandfather never kept anything that was worth giving away."[2]

The deepest value of our possessions remains underrated until they are unwrapped by those to whom we give them. Be generous; dare something bold for God. Christians should experience some perpetual discomfort over money and God, for this uneasiness will prompt you to draw closer to God, to discover new ways to make a difference, even to relish the deep wisdom of Merton's words: "If you have money, consider that perhaps the only reason God allowed it to fall into your hands was in order that you might find joy and perfection by giving it away."[3]

29

PSALM 62:1–2

For God alone my soul waits in silence; I shall not be greatly moved.

Faith waits. Faith is waiting, a patient stillness, a trust that trains binoculars toward the distance, watching for even a small movement, the subtle sign of God's action that comes in its own time. Faith is countercultural for us, largely because we hate waiting. We want to keep moving, we want it to happen now, we want to seize control. To be stuck in traffic, or a long grocery line, checking the time for an appointment that hasn't shown up, sitting in the doctor's waiting room, or hanging on through a long weekend wondering if it's malignant or benign: we cannot stand to wait, we want to get on with things, not to squander minutes needlessly, to fix things—now.

What are we waiting for, anyhow? My prince to come? The next big deal? Some dramatic turn of fortune? A quick resolution? Feeling better in five minutes? What would really satisfy? What is worth waiting for—if we could learn to wait?

St. Augustine began his spiritual autobiography by saying, "O Lord, you have made us for yourself, and our hearts are restless until they find rest in you."[1] Is my impatience, my inability to sit still, my frenetic round of busy-ness really an index into my lack of a sound relationship with God? Can I feel the itch inside, but then remember to calm down, realizing God is just beyond the horizon, coming, saving, loving—and all I need to do is to wait? My movement may plunge me into disaster; only God's movement matters. What happens "now" is gone by the next time I say "now." Our true life of togetherness with God is "now" only in God's good future. When I am in control, I get a lot of *me*; to let God be in control, I have to wait, to look and see, to expect something far greater than me. "They who wait for the LORD shall renew their strength" (Isa. 40:31).

Stillness not only places me squarely in the presence of God. Waiting on God also refurbishes the most essential virtue of the soul: commitment. I'm never sure if it's right to say, "We modern people are not good at commitment," or "We modern people are just committed to the wrong things." We flit about; the heat of the moment loosens what we thought we had glued down; feelings predictably ramble wildly, and we break commitments (and hearts). But when we are still, silent before God, when we wait only on God, we learn the secrets of "I shall not be moved," of commitment.

Lewis Smedes was right:

> Somewhere people still make and keep promises. They choose not to quit when the going gets rough. They stick to lost causes. They hold on to a love grown cold. If you have a ship you will not desert, if you have people you will not forsake, if you have causes you will not abandon, then you are like God. When a person makes a promise, she reaches out into an unpredictable future and makes one thing predictable: she will be there. . . . When you make a promise, you take a hand in creating your own future.[2]

Or in silent stillness you realize and implement the commitment of God's own future with you!

So this verse enacts a back-and-forth motion like a pendulum swinging, waiting for God, over to being committed, back to waiting, but with more good cause to wait now, over to a deepening commitment to the one who is unfailingly committed to us. After all, we have all the time in the world—in fact, all the time in eternity. A wait becomes an opportunity: instead of slamming your fists on the steering wheel, you fold those same hands and pray—which you probably think you don't have enough time for anyway, rushing around as you do. Someone's tardiness, a traffic snarl, or the other guy's incompetence that's making you wait can be transformed into a surprisingly lovely gift of a deeper awareness of God, who waits patiently on us, always.

Besides, we never fully seize God or the satisfactions of the Spirit now. We long for God, we yearn for what God will give, and so we wait, and the waiting becomes a delightful hankering, a joyful expectation. We do not demand that God act now or never.

And those who learn to wait can serve. In a restaurant, the "waiter" exists to serve others. His desires, her preferences, are beside the point. The waiter wants only to please the one dining. "For God alone my soul waits." In humility, firmly committed, we ask: "What can I get for you? How can I make your day better, O Lord?" No request is too grand. We place ourselves at God's disposal. We wait so we can wait. "They also serve who only stand and wait" (John Milton, "On His Blindness").

30

HEBREWS 4:15–16

For we have not a high priest who is unable to sympathize with our weaknesses, but one who in every respect has been tempted as we are, yet without sinning. Let us then with confidence draw near to the throne of grace, that we may find grace to help in time of need.

One after another through Israel's history, various men held the holiest office: that of high priest. Some were despised, others were beloved. Archaeologists have unearthed what they believe was the residence of the high priests—rather luxurious, not surprisingly, since many high priests were in collusion with the Roman overlords. The fate of all these priests was the same, though: the more spectacular but humbling archaeological find has been the fancy box that contained the bones of Caiaphas, the high priest at the time of Jesus' crucifixion.

Jesus had no lavish palace and left no bone box behind: Jesus "passed through the heavens" (Heb. 4:14). Although not one person thought of him as any kind of priest at all, he secretly fulfilled the office of high priest, representing us in God's presence, bridging the gulf between sinful humanity and God.

God could just forgive from on high, the way a flowing-robed judge might peer from his lofty perch behind a large wooden desk and utter a sentence. But God is better than that. God sent a priest who is able to sympathize with our weaknesses. Did the people feel the priests were remote and unsympathetic? Does God seem remote and unsympathetic? If we compare Christianity and the other religions of the world, our lone unique feature is that God came down, entered into our mortal frame, and experienced every temptation, every sorrow, yet also human delight and love, heartbreak and joy, and even the agony of death itself. Our inner turmoil, our dreams, our quirkiness, our woundedness: none of this is unfamiliar to our Lord, who knows us from the inside out and came to redeem it all.

For a moment, though, this verse seems to isolate us from Jesus: he was "without sin"? We say someone is "only human," meaning he is flawed or she bungled something. But Jesus was no less human for being sinless; the Christmas carol that says, "But little Lord Jesus, no crying he makes," is wrong. Jesus was sinless in that he never took his eye off God, his Father; he never "sinned," which we do when we say, "I am the center of the universe, I'll have it my way, I can go it on my own." At every huge turning point, and in every small moment, Jesus fixed his gaze on God, and on his mission to usher us into God's presence.

Was Jesus truly tested "in every respect"? Robertson Davies once joked that Jesus never had to deal with a difficult spouse! Yet Jesus knew women, probably better than we know women, or men. Jesus was so obsessed with God, and with other people, that he saw them more clearly than we see each other. He did, and now can "sympathize": break down the word, and we see it means "to suffer with." We never suffer alone; God is closest to us in our darkest moments.

Once as I visited a woman in the hospital, she reached up to hug me, pulled me down, and the tears running onto her cheeks were blotted onto my cheeks. When I raised back from her, she saw the tears, took a tissue, wiped them, and said, "Don't cry; it will be OK." My tears were first her tears; our tears are God's tears before they are our own.

So we may come before God with confidence. The Greek word *parresia* means "boldness, frankness, free speech." We can say quite literally anything, everything; God loves candor, and our intimacy with God is nothing less than a blabbering of every fear, whim, fantasy, hurt, confession, and delight, because God knows, Jesus has been there. And not only are we invited to voice all our feelings to God—the tears go both ways. We can feel what God feels and think God's thoughts. Perhaps we become like May, the young woman in *The Secret Life of Bees* whose twin sister died. They had been "like one soul sharing two bodies. If April got a toothache, May's gum would plump up red and swollen."[1] After April's death, "it seemed like the world itself became May's twin sister." Any word of anyone suffering struck agony into May's heart. All her family could do was to build a "wailing wall" in the back yard; May would write down the hurts of the world and people she knew on scraps of paper and press them into the wall.

We go to the wall to speak frankly with Jesus, who sympathizes. And we do not merely suffer with him; we "find grace to help in time of need." We know that we too will one day "pass through the heavens." St. Catherine of Siena imagined the wood of the cross as a bridge between our sorrowing lives and eternal life with God. So we are saved, not by a salvation tossed down from a distance, but from the inside. This is the help we need, the mercy we yearn for. And so when we face overwhelming challenges, we hold fast—and discover Christ holding fast to us.

31

EXODUS 20:9–10

*Remember the sabbath day, to keep it holy. Six days you
shall labor, but the seventh day is a sabbath to the LORD.*

The secret to finding God (or being found by God) is what
you do with precisely one seventh of your life. If God
feels like an absentee at work, or at play, or at home, maybe
it's because you never don't work—your motto is "work hard,
play hard"—or you're never at home. You may be in your house
from time to time. But do you ever come home to the God who
made you, for a much-needed rest?

God made the world, laboring hard for six days; then on the
seventh God rested. When God crafted you and me, he issued a
user's manual that says mercifully, "Six days you shall labor, but
the seventh is a sabbath to the LORD."

What if our days were not clumped into batches of seven?
Imagine the brutal grind of an endless succession of days if God
had not invented the "week"? Do I wish my week had nine or
ten or sixty days, so I could get more done? Or is it by the merciful, tender pity of God that I get only seven? or actually six?
God wired humanity in such a way that we are most fully the

people God made us to be when we count only six and keep a seventh for God.

Deep inside, aren't you weary? God foresaw that we would strangle our calendars full and become exhausted, so God lovingly permits rest. Rest is not laziness. Laziness is me being self-indulgent; rest is about God. The Sabbath isn't God frowning on you if you feel the urge to enjoy yourself; the Sabbath is God smiling on you, eager to have some quiet time with you. To observe the Sabbath is to say that not everything depends on me and my feverish activity; on the Sabbath we say, "God matters; nothing is so alluring that it could crowd out my special day with God. I really could use some rest."

Jesus said, "The sabbath was made for man, not man for the sabbath" (Mark 2:27). The Sabbath isn't a prison of rules; the Sabbath is "a banquet of time . . . the dessert we leave on the table."[1] It is a day of restoration, a day for healing, a day for your inner hunger to be satisfied.

If no time is sacred, if every day, every hour, is up for grabs, then nothing is sacred, and we get frazzled by a frantic, frivolous frenzy. If we could just sit down, turn the gadgets off, calm our minds, and just *be*—with ourselves, with each other, with God—for just a day, then the way yeast causes bread to rise we would discover a fullness to the entire week, maybe even a lifetime. Society calls Monday the first day of the week. But Christians have (ever since Jesus' tomb turned up empty) named Sunday the first day. It is in worship, rest, and solitude that I get my bearings on the week about to landslide over me. The first thing is God; I do not leave it to the last.

The constancy of weekly worship restores the image of God the world chips away at all week long. Annie Dillard once heard a minister, while leading worship, look up to the ceiling and say, "Lord, we say these same prayers every week!" After a pause, he continued; Dillard wryly adds, "Because of this, I like him very much."[2] Every week, we stop, we pray, we rest and do nothing much—except just being together, thinking and conversing about God, reflecting on life, noticing the sunset, picking a flower or two, taking a leisurely walk; we drink deeply from the water, store it up, and launch out into the week like a camel. These Sabbath delights are what give meaning to the rest of the week.

Walter Brueggemann wonderfully said that Jesus was using his "Sabbath voice"[3] when he said, "Come to me, all who labor and are heavy-laden, and I will give you rest" (Matt. 11:28). Jesus played a bit loose with the rules the pious Pharisees applied to the Sabbath, and they were annoyed that he "worked" on the holy day. But what was that "work"? Jesus didn't open his carpentry shop; he didn't dash off to pick up some fabric and detergent for his mother. He healed people who were sick and permitted his disciples to eat when they were desperately hungry. His rationale? "The sabbath was made for man, not man for the sabbath" (Mark 2:27).

On the Sabbath I declare that I am not ultimately determined by my productivity, my busy-ness, the round of diversions, what gets scribbled onto my calendar. I am God's child, I have a destiny far grander than this world's most soaring dream. To realize that destiny, I just have to be still, for a day, and to remember.

32

PSALM 119:105

Thy word is a lamp to my feet and a light to my path.

I once heard a talk in which the speaker began by quoting Emily Dickinson: "The unknown is the mind's greatest gift, and for it no one thinks to thank God." Since then, I have learned Dickinson didn't say this; but who did? The answer is unknown—a bit of ironic humor for such a shrewd saying.

Knowledge is good; more knowledge is always better. So how can the unknown be good? If I bother caring about what I do not know, then I have some homework ahead of me, I might honor somebody else by asking a question, I can't get cocky, the steel trapdoor can't shut on my soul.

Yes, in the rearview mirror we see our past and wish we had known some very important things: if I had known the Dow Jones would plummet . . . , if I had known he would break my heart . . . , if I had known cancer was growing . . . , if, if, if. George Eliot was wise, and sadly right, when she wrote, "Perhaps nothing would be a lesson to us if it didn't come too late."[1]

With God, what we do not know may be our richest spiritual treasure. "Faith is the assurance of things hoped for, the conviction of things not seen" (Heb. 11:1); "We walk by faith, not by sight" (2 Cor. 5:7). I want to know the future; but really what I need to do is trust God as I move into an unknown future. If I know, I jettison God, I dispense with the need for faith. Not knowing, I can plunge into the dark alone or tremble in fear — or I can step confidently, knowing God is with me.

"Thy word is a lamp." God's word helps me find my way in the dark and not get lost. Sometimes we want to know what God has in store next week, next month, next year, for the rest of my life. Why doesn't God reveal the whole blueprint right now? But how far can you see with just a lamp? In Bible times, to get around you had to carry fire, a torch, a lantern, or you'd fall on the rocks or traipse off into a hole. And with a Bronze Age lantern — not one of those brilliant outdoor beacons campers use nowadays — how far ahead could you see? Not far. But far enough. You see well enough to take the next step, and the next step. The end of the road is all darkness. But it will be lit when you get near enough.

God does not encourage us to see too far ahead; God's will is a relationship. If I spend a day in the Appalachian Mountains with my wife, I am not sure whether she will want to hike a trail on the Blue Ridge Parkway or stop off at the Folk Art Center. But I never get lost. I just stick near her. The thrill is in not being so certain. We go here now, and I trust her with wherever we wind up next.

So it is with God. What is faith? Knowing and agreeing to everything in advance? God called Abraham: "Go from your country . . . to the land that I will show you" (Gen. 12:1). Which land might that be? God did not show him just yet. Jesus walked up to some fishermen, and out of the blue he said, "Put down your nets and follow me" (Matt. 4:19). Where? They did not know yet. But they went wherever Jesus went; their path was defined not by destination but by proximity to Jesus, who kept moving around.

Where will God lead you and me? We do now know yet. Faith is risky: we leave the cocoon of our preplanned, carefully managed lives and go—where? We do not know yet. Wherever God leads, that is where we will go. But we know whom we are following, and we want to be near him, and that is enough, for he is the fullness of life; he is the way, the truth, and the life.

So along the way, you have to do some trusting. Each step is a step of faith—which leads me to a second thing: What is the lamp to my feet? God's word. How much light is there in a word? Can you see a word? Words are not solid, they shed no real light—but they are what we need on the journey. The psalmist, I think, imagines God speaking gently to us, over and over: "Here, this way, ooh, watch out, good job, over here, step up, keep coming, stop for a minute, rest awhile, get moving now, hurry through here . . . " The invisible word becomes the sure light.

How do we hear this word? God speaks, and God speaks primarily through the Bible—and we familiarize ourselves with the cadence and accent of God's voice by hearing it over and over, reading, studying, reflecting with others. Then, on that dark night, and even in the broad light of day, we have God guiding us as we move forward, telling us only what we need to know right now, for the very next step.

I think the unknown really is the mind's greatest gift—and for it, and for the small flicker of light that really is enough to take the next step, we will give thanks to God.

33

JAMES 1:22

Be doers of the word, and not hearers only.

Words. So many of them out there, flying about, none car-
rying much freight, as light as straw. Yes, occasionally a
word matters. For Christians, words matter, and we even call
the ultimate manifestation of who God is the "Word made flesh."

And yet, a nagging uneasiness hounds us, the foreboding
that Christianity will be nothing but words, just so much talk,
of no real substance. Our faith can be something flimsy pasted
on the outside of an otherwise unchanged life. Words that matter actually change things. If the Word made flesh matters, if the
Word of God is worth attending to, then it issues in a changed
life, altered behavior, radical acts of compassion and hospitality,
holiness, generosity, a tangible goodness.

James warns us that faith without works is dead (Jas. 2:17);
his counsel, of which we should remind ourselves daily, hourly,
minutely, secondly, is "Be doers of the word, and not hearers
only." We need a little more "doing" of the faith, don't we—especially in a world that is cynical about Jesus and the Church? G.

K. Chesterton was right: it is not that Christianity has been tried and found wanting; it has hardly been tried at all. Jesus did not come so we could *feel* different; he came so we could *be* different.

But aren't we saved by faith, not our works? Wasn't the apostle Paul's entire mission to declare salvation by grace, that the largest achievable mountain of fantastic good deeds cannot shove us into heaven? Indeed. But Paul was obsessed with changed behavior, Paul was adamant about holiness, Paul collected money from the poor to keep the desperately poor alive. Paul and James had met and seemed to celebrate the notion that one enjoyed a special divine vocation to emphasize grace, the other an equally special vocation to emphasize what the results of that grace might look like. Richard Bauckham imagined what an ongoing conversation between the hero of faith and the champion of works might look like: "There would be much nodding of heads and smiling agreement, as well as some knitting of brows and some exclamations of surprise."[1]

Nonetheless, Martin Luther was so annoyed by the letter of James he mockingly dubbed it the "epistle of straw." But Luther's problem, and the problem of Christians he saw daily, was different from ours: they were obsessed with God's will, they fretted anxiously over whether they were doing enough for God, they wrung their hands in fear that they weren't holy enough. We, on the other hand, hardly think twice about holiness, we assume God must really adore "nice" people like us, and we are obsessed with ourselves and prefer a God who will give us a well-deserved boost along the way. Do people like us really need to hear more from Paul, suggesting our works don't matter and we are saved by grace? Is this word of grace an immense relief to us who have no works to boast of? Or does grace become a sense of entitlement?

But then we do good things. In fact, sometimes we identify being a Christian with little acts of charity: Christians donate to the food drive, we send shoes to Kenya, we help paint a clinic or the Sunday school room—and so our faith must be sound, since we have done some things. Aren't we in some danger of doing, and doing, and doing, so that all our doing is no more than trying to stay in control of our own existence, masking an inability to receive unconditional love, to rest in God's grace?

What if it turns out that the James who wrote this "epistle of straw" was, as many scholars think, the brother of Jesus? What could be more persuasive, what case for Christ could be more compelling, than that his little brother became a follower and thought of Jesus not only as his big brother but as his Lord, as Savior of the world? Siblings quibble, have to be told to share their toys, know one another's foibles. James knew Jesus all his life, and if we want to talk about having a "relationship" with Jesus, who better to learn from than James? Families are all grace, and all doing too. You stick with whom you're stuck with in a family, so it's grace, and yet in a family you help with the chores or nurse ailing parents; you share the gritty tasks of daily survival.

Perhaps James is inviting us, not to prove our faith in God with a pile of good deeds, but to be in a family, to love Jesus and those he loved, to stand shoulder to shoulder and share the labor, to do what we say matters to each other in this marvelous, quirky, dysfunctional but enduring family. Words enacted in mundane life. In Jesus' house in Nazareth, do you know what you had to put on the floor, and in the mouths of the animals just outside the door? Straw. The stuff of family.

34

PHILIPPIANS 2:6–7

*Have this mind among yourselves, which you have in
Christ Jesus, who, though he was in the form of God, did
not count equality with God a thing to be grasped, but
emptied himself, taking the form of a servant.*

I recall reading somewhere, back when I was in seminary, that
Philippians 2:5–11 was an early Christian hymn. I hope so.
To imagine the first Christians, with no curriculum, no hym-
nals, no theological libraries, before the great church councils,
when only a handful of enthusiastic oddballs knew anything at
all about Christianity, not only spoke but lifted their voices in
song to praise Jesus as emptying himself of equality with God:
how lovely, how profound, how pregnant with hope even now!

In the Roman world, as in our world, people raced for hon-
ors, strove gamely on a hopefully upwardly mobile course in
life, seizing power, cash, and possessions any way they could.
Jesus bolted against the norm and took a downwardly mobile
path. With the power that hurled the universe into being at his
fingertips, Jesus did not exploit what he had at his disposal but
poured himself out, refused to dazzle the crowds with impres-
siveness, took towel and basin and washed feet, ate with the
lowly and despised.

But let us not think "How marvelous that Jesus jettisoned his might and embarked upon a strange mission that must have been as difficult for him as my plunging into a mission junket to the poorest place on earth!" Jesus' mission was no anomaly; God was not pretending or playing a role onstage, or temporarily suspending divine power. What we see in Jesus is precisely who God truly is, what God always has been, and how God always will act. It is always in the very nature of God to pour out, to empty the divine self, to serve.

In fact, many scholars of Paul dare to translate Philippians 2:6–7 not as "Though he was in the form of God, [he] emptied himself," but rather, "Because he was in the form of God he emptied himself." Indeed. It was precisely because he fully was God and transparently unveiled the heart of God that Jesus came as a humble nobody and consorted with nobodies and laid down his life, bearing shame and abandoning all privilege. Michael Gorman called the cross "the signature of the Eternal One."[1] When God created everything, it was not a brandishing of might, however mind-boggling the process of creating billions of galaxies might be; rather, God simply emptied God's own self, God stooped down to serve, and the lavish universe was lifted up from the ash heap. If we could peer through the Hubble telescope or some time-travel machine back into the very moment of creation itself, would there not be a God emptying God's self, humbly, serving, perhaps with a pair of crossed timbers the first matter to emerge from nothingness?

How do we respond to such a self-emptying God? Yes, we try to imitate, we start giving our stuff away and do what we can selflessly for others. But the Gospel isn't that Jesus came and died so that you might be unselfish. Pagans might be unselfish. Jesus came so we might be his friends, so we might have our feet washed by him, so we might quite simply be with him, rest near him, and love him. We might just contemplate Jesus, perhaps in the form of some icon, those artistic creations of believers who thought it worthwhile just to stare at Jesus for a while. Or we might sing a hymn or two, such as "When I Survey the Wondrous Cross" or "How Great Thou Art": "When I survey the wondrous cross On which the Prince of glory died, My richest gain I count but loss. . . . Were the whole realm of nature mine, That were a present far too small"; or "O Lord my God, . . . I see the stars, . . . from lofty mountain grandeur . . . and when I think that God, His Son not sparing, sent Him to die, I scarce can take it in."

And we pray, not for Christ to drop down or mail in some blessing from that cross. We seek union with him. Near the end of his life, St. Francis of Assisi began praying these words:

> Lord, two graces I ask before I die:
> One is that I may feel in my soul and body
> the sorrow you underwent in your most holy passion.
> The second is that I may feel in my soul and body
> the love with which you were inflamed so as to undergo
>   such a death for us.[2]

He saw the form of God and did not wish for any distance between his form, the shape of his life, mind, and heart and that of Jesus. We yearn for oneness with God, to mirror the form of Jesus that he exhibited precisely because he was in the form of God.

35

1 SAMUEL 1:15

I am a woman sorely troubled; I have drunk neither wine nor strong drink, but I have been pouring out my soul before the LORD.

Once the center of gravity in Israel's political and religious life, Shiloh is now little more than some old rocks, an intriguing archaeological site, in a barren expanse of land few visit. Among the stones, scholars can detect the city gate, dwellings, and perhaps the altar. What is harder to detect is the personal drama, the heartbreak, love, grief, laughter, dreams, and faith that made the place what it was.

How poignant is the story in 1 Samuel 1? Hannah was unable to bear children—her frustration made worse by her husband's other wife, who snidely mocked her. When they went up to worship at Shiloh, Hannah prayed; her womb was empty, but her soul was rich. Her prayer was neither polite nor mere rote recitation; her supplication wasn't lifted from a book or hurried. She dared to look into the marrow of her being, and she let the tears, hopes, disappointments flow—nothing hidden, nothing harbored. So absorbed was she in her praying that Eli, the priest, presumed she was drunk—reminding us of the first Christians on the day of Pentecost (Acts 2:13)!

Alcohol is a pervasive problem, and many Christians drink too much or don't know how to have fun without drinking. But the image is arresting, as Frederick Buechner realized: "Wine is dangerous; it makes the timid brave and the reserved amorous. It loosens the tongue and breaks the ice; it kills germs."[1] Prayer can be when the timid become brave, when your reserve melts into love; your tongue is loosened . . . and you pour out, not what you think God wants to hear, but what is really in the depths of your heart. Instead of lashing out or feeling sorry for herself, Hannah prayed, not pouring wine into her mouth to allay her grief, but pouring out her heart to God.

Her prayers remind us of those of another woman: Monica, mother of St. Augustine. Her son was grown but showed no signs of commitment to Christ, and his lifestyle was troubling. Monica prayed as intently as Hannah; Ambrose, the priest, witnessed her profound supplications and declared, "It is not possible that the child of so many tears could be lost."

Eli was moved by Hannah's prayer and assured her that God would hear. When she prayed to give birth to a child, her wish was not "so I can have a child and be fulfilled." Instead, she pledged that if she had a child she would consecrate that child to God's service. Hannah would prefer to clutch her son tightly and keep him for herself. But she sees him as a precious gift from God—and gives him back to God. Whatever you and I have that is good: we would be wise to promise it to God before we get it, when we get it, and when we remember that we got it. Then, and only then, will we experience in our hearts the joy and delight Hannah sang to her God.

Could it be we might rethink why we have children—not for ourselves, but to commit that child to God? Could it be that the hidden purpose of a family is not to be "happy," but to live out a passionate devotion to God?

Sometimes in obituaries, I read about an older woman of immense faith. When her "survivors" are listed—a son, a granddaughter—I think, "Yes, he survived, and so did she, probably because of the treasury of prayers offered up by this one who has died; imagine how many times, and with how much love, she had prayed for them!"

In many communities, school systems are political battle-grounds: people grouse about budgets, and education gets politicized like everything else. But what if the people of faith, daily and with largehearted determination, prayed for the children (and teachers, administrators, drivers, support staff)?

I read a study involving two hospitals that indicated "Prayer works." Holy people prayed for patients in one hospital but not the other, and the prayed-for patients showed slight improvement. We're glad to hear this! What if we conducted a serious test of prayer involving two schools? But instead of praying for one and not the other, we pray for both?

Pray for the school that serves your neighborhood, but then pray for another elsewhere in the city, where prayer might be the last best hope on earth for God's children. Then we might hear God's voice, just as Hannah heard Eli's, offering words of hope—or more likely words of challenge: "Keep praying, but then ask if you, or your Church family, might be the answer to your own prayers for the children."

36

⌒⌒⌒

2 KINGS 5:1

Naaman, commander of the army of the king of Syria,
was a mighty man of valor, but he was a leper.

The very thought of Baptism makes me shudder. I remember mine, since my parents didn't take me to be sprinkled as an infant. At age eight, terrified by a Baptist preacher, I sprinted to the altar to avoid the flames of hell. In short order, I found myself donning waders in a bathtub-like pool behind the choir. The minister hoisted me backward, dunking my head underwater not once, but thrice—which sent me flailing, embarrassing myself and the brimstone preacher.

Embarrassment is simply the nervous side of humility. Humility is hard, but it is simply the truth about us. Yes, Naaman was a man of valor, of substance. *But* . . . there is always a "but" isn't there? *But* he was a leper. Greatness, or pretended greatness, inevitably encounters humility. Naaman is great, *but* . . . his unwelcomed humility is mirrored to him in the person of a young woman, small of stature (and female!); he is a captain, she a captive. All other healers having failed him, Naaman is desperate enough to follow her tip: the not-yet-humbled

Naaman rumbles up to Elisha's house, reining in his stallions, bearing gifts, expecting to pay his way to healing. A price is to be exacted from Naaman, but it is his own humility.

Elisha is unimpressed. After all, once you've seen chariots and horses blazing with fire, riding not across rugged terrain but soaring above the clouds (2 Kings 2), a bunch of steeds pulling a cocky chieftain atop wooden wheels just doesn't raise your pulse. Not deigning to come out, Elisha disses Naaman, enraging him. Naaman was prideful, but perhaps pride was all he had left. Much as we might do in the privacy of the doctor's or therapist's office, we've dressed well, and we mention some cool thing we did last night — but obviously we have come not for banter, but to be healed, to reveal the "but," to expose what hinders us, hoping, blushing. The "but," the wound, is the shutter thrown open to receive the morning sun.

How fascinating: Elisha could have come out; he could have made the trip himself to Damascus; he could have healed at a distance. But he lets Naaman come to him. When Joseph's brothers were hungry, he could have shipped food to them, but he let them come. Joseph didn't want them merely to fill their bellies; he wanted to heal the relationship. Elisha doesn't want Naaman merely to be rid of leprosy; he wants him to be more deeply healed. By not even paying him the courtesy of coming to the door, Elisha reverses the sorry tale Jesus would tell of a rich man not coming to the door to help out a poor leper (Luke 16:19–31)!

Elisha's prescription isn't courteous, either: bathe in the Jordan. Pilgrims to Israel chuckle when they see the Jordan, hardly a river at all, more of a stream, a creek. Naaman protests: Shouldn't his cure be more dazzling, perhaps dipping himself in the pools by the Hanging Gardens of Babylon? or some exotic salve imported from Ethiopia?

Faith is the crumpling of pride, best achieved through something as simple, as obvious, as unimpressive as a bit of water only Elisha or somebody desperately thirsty would think of as powerful. I do not know if Naaman flailed a bit trying to get his whole body under such a shallow, coursing stream. But we know there was a miracle in that water. Sure, the leprosy washed downstream. Yet, more importantly, when he stepped up onto the riverbank, drenched and dripping, he was no longer merely a man, but somehow like a boy: "his flesh was restored like the flesh of a little child," like the little maiden who showed him the way, like all of us when we "become like children."

All of Christianity is a kind of return to childhood, a training in humility. All our gestures seem silly: folding our hands, bowing our heads, kneeling. How do you get ahead or defend yourself acting in these ways? We believe in vulnerability, humility, a bit of flailing in embarrassment. Dipping in a no-account river on the suggestion of a two-bit prophet who wouldn't even answer the door: the foolishness of God is wiser than all of us.

The humility goes on. Sensing that his newfound excitement about God will be compromised once he returns home, Naaman rather charmingly scoops up some dirt to carry back with him, to cling to some piece of holiness in an unholy place. Our post-baptized life is full of dilemmas and difficulties; not surprisingly we fail miserably. We cannot heal ourselves or achieve what God wants of us. But we remember the water, the awkward humiliation—and wasn't it precisely at that moment of spiraling out of control, of losing all hope and dignity, that a slight rustling of wings and a whispered message were heard, something like "This is my beloved child," just a boy, a girl, small, wet, like we were at birth, like we will be when we are greeted at the door by fiery chariots?

37

JOHN 14:6

Jesus said, "I am the way, and the truth, and the life; no one comes to the Father, but by me."

E-mail has the same problem as the Bible: you can never pick up tone of voice or facial expressions. When Jesus said, "I am the way, and the truth, and the life," were his words punctuated, firm, brows furrowed, using his hands to narrow the scope? Or was he tender, hands outstretched, his heart almost breaking? We Christians have this notoriously bad habit of taking the words of the Bible and twisting them into a barbed-wire fence, to protect ourselves and shut others out, instead of letting God's Word manifest itself as a window flung open, the arms of God's love embracing us. What prompted Jesus to say, "I am the way, and the truth, and the life"? and what might it mean for us?

Consider the context. Jesus is not delivering a dogmatic lecture or conducting a discussion group on the relationship between Christianity and world religions. He has just finished an ominous dinner, his last with his beloved friends, the room thick with fear and sorrow. He has just washed the confused disciples' feet; they are dazed, forlorn, dimly aware he is about to leave them, and they don't know whether to cling doggedly to him or flee for the exits. To his companions riddled with gloom, Jesus begins: "Let not your hearts be troubled. . . . I go to prepare a place for you." But they plead with him: "We do not know the way."

By "way" they don't mean the one and only thought pattern that purchases salvation; they mean a road, a door. And Jesus, typically (just as he had said "I am the light of the world" to people groping in the dark, "I am the bread of life" to people hungry for bread, "I am the living water" to those with a gnawing thirst in their gut) says, "I am the way. Stay close to me, I am the road, the door."

I do not believe Jesus was slamming the security gates of heaven shut to keep the riffraff out. I believe he was comforting the hopeless, by saying, "Don't despair: there *is* a way. You aren't stuck down here with nothing but your own resources — I am God come down to carry you on the wings of grace to your destiny." When we listen to Jesus, when we gaze into his heart, and mind, we see clearly the character, heart, and very being of God. Jesus is not only the way, but also the truth (in a world of lies and deception) and the life (in the realm where death seems to trump in with the final word).

All religions are not the same; not all paths to God are valid. Jesus is the pure, eternally intended revelation of God, the embodied mercy of God. Philip asks him, "Show us the Father," and Jesus did by simply standing there, but then by washing their feet, praying in Gethsemane, forgiving his executioners, extending mercy to a common criminal, dying, ushering us into the presence of God. He indeed is the way. "No one comes to the Father, but by me."

But notice: Jesus did not say, "No one comes to the Father but by that person's faith, spirituality, moral rectitude, right thinking about God, or Church membership." We get confused, and think salvation comes by *my* stellar decision for God. We are saved by God, not by our religiosity, however noble. We are saved by grace, the free, unmerited favor of God. If this is so, was Jesus saying only Christians who think the right things about him are saved? Wasn't Jesus extending his arms as wide as the world—as wide as the cross? And isn't that precisely why he is the way?

I do not believe Jesus intended to define ultimate truth about salvation in these words of John 14:6—although I do believe he is the inescapable truth about God and the way God saves people and the world. But how then do we think about people who don't believe in Christ, who embrace other faiths, who could care less? Hans Urs von Balthasar wrote an insightful book called *Dare We Hope that All Men Will Be Saved?* He does not claim that everyone will be saved; but he says the Christian has no other option but to *hope* every person will be saved. No one is dispensable—we never look at him or her or them and say, "They are toast." We believe passionately in Jesus; therefore we see even the most vehement unbeliever as someone loved profoundly by God; we hope God will save that person. We do not carry the responsibility to decide, but we must and may always hope.

Might it be that Jesus is the way even for some who don't accept him—for all sorts of odd reasons, from never having heard about Jesus to only hearing about Jesus from vile people? In his classic *Mere Christianity*, C. S. Lewis wrote, "The truth is, God has not told us what His arrangements about other people are. We do know that no man can be saved except through Christ; we do not know that only those who know Him can be saved through Him."[1] Is this nonsense? Perhaps—but we hope not. We are the people Jesus taught to hope, to have pure hearts, to get so close to him in his mercy that we become mercy and hope ourselves.

38

MATTHEW 2:1

When Jesus was born in Bethlehem of Judea, in the days of Herod the king, behold, wise men from the East came to Jerusalem.

If you've sat through enough Christmas pageants, it may be hard to banish the image of would-be magi wearing bathrobes and Burger King crowns, trying to appear wise and regal. But Matthew's magi would have been exotic novelties in a backwater like Bethlehem. Who were these travelers from faraway Persia, who studied star charts and discerned fates in the night sky? Who could be less likely to have discovered the Christ child? Their mystical craft, handed down from the ancient Sumerians, was regarded by Judaism and then Christianity as bogus, even dangerous. Instead of waiting expectantly for some Messiah, they were taking notes on comets and planetary movements. Yet they are the ones who have come to worship the Messiah.

What did they see? A supernova? Jupiter and Saturn in conjunction? A comet? How would a star point to a particular house anyhow? Medieval writers believed the magi saw a bright angel, which they mistook for a star, who led them directly to the manger.[1]

Matthew isn't endorsing astrology. Instead, he cleverly testifies to the power of God, not merely to bring into the fold those who have until now been clueless about God's plan, but even to manipulate nature itself. God is "the love that moves the stars" (as Dante[2] put it). St. Augustine wrote, "Christ was not born because the star shone forth, but it shone forth because Christ was born; we should say not that the star was fate for Christ, but that Christ was fate for the star."[3] So, we are not the star-crossed victims of fate. This newborn Jesus is our destiny.

The tragic comedy of this story? Herod's Scripture experts had scrolls, but they missed the Messiah's birth—and when they got a whiff that the Scripture might actually be taking on flesh, they recoiled and lashed out defensively. Today, we might notice who "gets" Jesus and who doesn't, and ask: Do we ever hold the truth in our hands but miss the living Lord? God is determined to be found and will use any and all measures, even what is tomfoolery, to reach out to people who are open.

Who is King? And who isn't? Herod isn't, although he brandishes the gaudy symbols of kingship. Herod was history's most hysterical megalomaniac: massive ego, paranoid, and brutally violent. The magi were lucky to get away after saying to his face, "Where is the king of the Jews? We have come to worship him." The irony was as rich as when a grown-up Jesus was asked by Pontius Pilate, "Are you a king?" (John 18:33). When the first Christians declared "Jesus is Lord," the implication was "Caesar isn't." Jesus was not a military subversive trying to take over the empire. But he was king, and Herod, Pilate, and Caesar were exposed as mere pretenders.

If Jesus is king, there is something upside down and just plain unkingly about him. His courtiers were poor fishermen, his standard a cross, his boast not ironfisted dominance but tender love. Little wonder Herod was "troubled." All who cling to power, who lust for dominance, are in for a headlong tumble before this Christ child.

Theologically, manger scenes and Christmas pageants can be problematical. Surveying the scene, a child would quite naturally identify with Jesus. I am the child, and there's Mary and

Joseph, just like my mom and dad. The magi have come bringing gifts—to *me*! Just like Santa Claus. Christmas becomes for most of us a grand festival of gift giving, a frenzy of gift receiving. But the gifts of the magi aren't little child-appropriate presents for Jesus to enjoy. They are symbolic of the grandeur of creation being gathered at the feet of the Lord of it all.

Do the three gifts symbolize anything? Theologians have guessed: gold reflects Jesus' royalty, frankincense his divinity, myrrh his sorrowful death to come. Did God whisper to the magi back in Persia so they would know what symbolic gifts to bring? They simply brought what was precious, what they wanted the Lord to have.

The magi didn't need to be warned in a dream not to revisit the villainous Herod! Yet an angel—perhaps the same one who brightly led them there in the first place?—warned them to take an evasive route. They departed "by another way." Could it be that Matthew is offering a tantalizing hint about life for those who've met Christ? You abandon the old road. You unfold a new map and discover an alternate path.

T. S. Eliot imagined the thoughts of the magi back home: "We returned to our places . . . , But no longer at ease here, in the old dispensation, With an alien people clutching their gods."[4] Jesus doesn't make my life more comfortable; Jesus doesn't help me fit in and succeed. We are no longer at ease in a world not committed to Jesus; we notice false gods and royal pretenders all over the place. Nothing is the same. An alternate road is now our path—but the road is going somewhere.

39

LUKE 2:34

This child is set for the fall and rising of many in Israel.

A few days after Jesus was born, Mary and Joseph dutifully took their son to the Temple to fulfill the letter of Jewish law, and their diligence raises questions for Christians who feel no obligation to Judaism or the Old Testament's laws. More personally, we see a family bringing their newborn child to the temple to make—a sacrifice? In our comfortable world, parents and newborn usually *receive* gifts instead of making them: an office shower, savings bonds from grandparents, cute alumni bibs. What if we sacrificed something of immense value to mark a birth, to consecrate a child to God?

The purpose of the sacrifice? "For their purification" (Luke 2:22). But there was no need for this child to be purified. No need for Mary (whom Wordsworth called "our tainted nature's solitary boast"[1]) to be purified either. Karl Barth rather wonderfully wrote that, when Jesus was baptized, he needed to be washed of sin—not *his* sin, but *our* sin: "No one who came to the Jordan was as laden and afflicted as He."[2] No one ever came to the temple for purification as laden with sin—not his, or his mother's, but ours—as Jesus.

Because of his purifying mission, Jesus truly is, as Oscar Hijuelos phrased it, "the most wanted child in the history of the world."[3] How lovely the way Simeon, the frailties of his years draped over him, cradles the infant Jesus in his arms. Imagine: holding in your arms this most wanted child, the hope of the ages, the yearning of your entire life.

But Jesus was just a baby! God became small to win our hearts. Infants wield immense power. Muscular men with callused hands become gentle as pillows when handed a baby; potent people with gruff voices adopt a falsetto and coo at the sight of an infant. God came down not to thrash evildoers. God came down as a mere infant, to elicit love, to nurture tenderness.

Simeon had waited all his life for this child. We do not like to wait. We want to move, stay in control, make it happen, rush to the next titillation—and in our inability to be still and know that God is God, we miss God. "They who wait for the LORD shall renew their strength" (Isa. 40:31).

God is not a possession you nab and cling to *now*. God is like a lover at some distance. You are filled with longing—and it is the longing that is sweet, dizzying, delightful in anticipation, rippling with eagerness. Gregory of Nyssa understood yearning for God: "constantly going on in the quest and never ceasing in ascent, seeing that every fulfillment . . . continually generates a further desire." This discovery, "far from making the soul despair, is actually an experience of God's fuller presence."[4]

Because of this child, Simeon can die calmly, confidently. He can be as hospitable to his impending death as he has been to the child Mary brought to the temple, embracing it, blessing God for it. Then we see Anna too, quite old, having led an uneventful life, focused on only one vista, God's salvation. God's blessing was not a continual smorgasbord of titanic experiences and shiny baubles. God's blessing was just one thing, and it was eighty years coming. "Purity of heart is to will one thing" (Søren Kierkegaard);[5] "One thing is needful" (Luke 10:42), to be near Jesus, to see salvation dawn. It is enough.

Just a child—but not really safe and harmless: "This child is set for the fall and rising of many." This child provokes a crisis, a decision, for Simeon, for Anna, for all people of every generation. How we respond to this one person decides everything. The stakes are not trivial. It is not that, if we go with Jesus, our lives are 17 percent better, our happiness 14 percent higher, our marriages 16 percent healthier. It's all or nothing. You fall, or you rise.

Notice the order. In the world, it's the rise and fall of the Third Reich, the rise and fall of a movie star. But with Jesus it's *fall and rise*. "Unless a [seed] falls into the earth and dies, it remains alone; but if it dies, it bears much fruit" (John 12:24). Anna fasts "night and day," not "day and night." Jesus did not fly directly up into heaven once danger flared. He suffered and died and then was raised to glory. We suffer and die—and not just at the end of life. I am "crucified with Christ" (Gal. 2:20); we bear the death of Christ now. We fall, and from that lowest point, we rise. We may just fall; but if we rise, we fall and then rise.

Perhaps Mary shuddered at Simeon's words. Mysteriously he spoke of "a sword piercing through [her] soul." It is moving to think of Mary, feeling Jesus kicking in her womb, hearing his first cry, nursing him, watching his first steps, hearing his first words. He grew strong, left home, and marshaled a following. But wicked men turned against her son, who was all pure, all good, all love. Mary had to watch as Simeon's prophecy was fulfilled. Her heart broke as she saw the lifeblood she had given him drain out of his beautiful body. The fall. But then the rise. Who, among all who witnessed Jesus risen from the dead, was more joyful to see him alive than his own mother?

40

PSALM 97:1

The LORD reigns; let the earth rejoice.

We have a little cluster of Psalms (93 through 99) whose primary theme is "The LORD reigns! The LORD is King!" Worshipers in ancient Israel must have had considerable chutzpah to travel for miles in caravans over rocky, dangerous terrain to press with the crowd into the Temple to shout "The Lord is King!" History seemed not to be on their Lord's side, as all the vast territories, tax revenues, and military victories were concentrated in the hands of the gods of Babylon, or Egypt, or Greece, or Rome, or any of a long parade of the truly high and mighty.

Their God (whose name was Yahweh) must have seemed like the weakling on the playground of bigger, more impressive deities (like Marduk or Ea of the mighty Babylonians, or Osiris or Horus of the wealthy Egyptians). All other gods could boast of military triumphs, vast hordes of gold, shinier cultic objects; if success was the measure, the gods of the Assyrians or the Phoenicians or just about anybody else had superior reasons to elicit praise from their subjects. Psalm 97 says, "Let the earth rejoice"—but I imagine the rest of the earth smirked, chuckled in ridicule, when Israel gathered to sing that Israel's Lord was king.

Why this foolishness in Israel? Was it lunacy? or a profound faith that could stand boldly in the face of being small, puny, a laughingstock, and still affirm that "Our Lord is King!—and yours isn't"? Did they understand the true nature of the true God? I suspect they did, though it was when Jesus arrived that the world was treated to the ultimate display of what exactly a King looks like. Jesus lay in a manger instead of a palace. Jesus surrounded himself with poor, clueless fishermen instead of a slick bureaucracy. Jesus recruited an army of grateful lepers instead of well-drilled regiments. Jesus rode a wobbly donkey instead of a sprightly stallion. Jesus assumed a cross instead of a throne, a crown of thorns, not gold and jewels.

Laugh out loud when the magi tell King Herod, "We have come to worship the king" (Matt. 2:2)—a rather rude affront to the guy sitting in the palace. Furrow your brow when Pontius Pilate snidely asks Jesus, "So you are a king?" (John 18:37). He commands no regiments, he calls down no heavenly power to defend himself, he says not a single word. In his entourage were not senators and oligarchs, but lepers, prostitutes, the unlettered, the nobodies. His monuments were sorrow and love that flow mingled down. At a crossroads he hangs on an olive shaft, a placard of mockery posted above his head in multiple languages so all can chuckle or scratch their heads in wonder, or perhaps even believe. Let earth receive her king.

Christians who strive for power in America or any other place on earth misconstrue the heart of our faith. We are historically wary of power: when J.R.R. Tolkien told his scintillating stories of the hobbits in *The Lord of the Rings* and their quest not to possess the ring of power but to destroy it, he articulated in fable form the essence of Christianity, which is not about our wielding power. We yield to the power of God, which is itself a small, paradoxical power, the power of humble service.

Or perhaps wisdom intuits that with our God we glimpse a very different, and much better, type of royalty. "The word of the cross is folly to those who are perishing, but to us who are being saved it is the power of God" (1 Cor. 1:18). Want to see power? Watch Jesus touch the untouchables or wash the feet of those who would gladly have washed his. Watch Jesus surrender his very life, so powerful was his love. Watch Jesus forgive the very people who just spat on him and drove nails into his flesh. Watch Jesus breathe his last—and then quite fantastically show up three days later. "The LORD reigns! Let the earth rejoice."

The world still mockingly laughs—or yawns. But we know, and we pray and praise the Lord, who is king. "Let the earth rejoice": we pray that they will, and until they do, we rejoice for them, on their behalf, raising a chorus of "Joy to the world. . . . Let earth receive her King" on behalf of those who are tone-deaf, who have not yet grasped the true nature of power, the wonder of love become flesh.

NOTES

1. John 1:14

1. David Bentley Hart, *The Beauty of the Infinite* (Grand Rapids: Eerdmans, 2003), 126.
2. David McCullough, *The Course of Human Events* (New York: Simon & Schuster, 2004), audiobook.

2. Matthew 18:3

1. Martin Luther quoted in Roland H. Bainton, *Here I Stand* (New York: Mentor, 1950), 236.
2. Charles Péguy, *The Mystery of the Holy Innocents*, tr. Pansy Pakenham (New York: Harper & Brothers, 1956), 135; quoted in Martin E. Marty, *The Mystery of the Child* (Grand Rapids: Eerdmans, 2007), 12.
3. Walter Hooper, *C. S. Lewis: A Companion & Guide* (San Francisco: HarperCollins, 1996), 397.
4. Neil Postman, *The Disappearance of Childhood* (New York: Vintage, 1982), 120.
5. Marty, *Mystery of the Child*, 17, 25, and passim.
6. Hans Urs von Balthasar, *Unless You Become like This Child*, trans. Erasmo Leiva-Merikakis (San Francisco: Ignatius, 1991), 49.

3. 2 Chronicles 20:12

1. Scott Bader-Saye, *Following Jesus in a Culture of Fear* (Grand Rapids: Brazos, 2007), 56.
2. Thomas Merton, *Thoughts in Solitude* (New York: Noonday, 1956), 83.

4. Genesis 28:16

1. Oscar Romero, *The Violence of Love* (Farmingham: Plough Publishing House, 1998), 131.
2. Hans Urs von Balthasar, *Prayer* (San Francisco: Ignatius, 1986), 23.
3. Thomas Merton, *Thoughts in Solitude* (New York: Noonday, 1956), 99.

5. Psalm 118:24

1. Arthur Miller, *After the Fall* (New York: Viking Press, 1964), 4.
2. Mother Teresa, *A Simple Path* (New York: Ballantine, 1995), 35.
3. Dietrich Bonhoeffer, *Life Together*, trans. John W. Doberstein (New York: Harper & Brothers, 1954), 43.

6. Psalm 121:3

1. John Henry Newman, *Selected Sermons, Prayers, and Devotions* (New York: Vintage, 1999), 385.

7. Psalm 19:14

1. Dietrich Bonhoeffer, *Life Together*, trans. John W. Doberstein (New York: Harper & Brothers, 1954), 91.
2. Jim Forest, "Dorothy Day," *The Encyclopedia of American Catholic History*, ed. Michael Glazier and Thomas J. Shelley (Collegeville, MN: Liturgical, 1991), 414.
3. Thomas Merton, *New Seeds of Contemplation* (New York: New Directions, 1961), 43, 16.

9. Philippians 4:6

1. Isaac Bashevis Singer, interview by Phyllis Malamud, October 5, 1978, "An Interview with Isaac Bashevis Singer," Library of America, http://singer100.loa.org/life/commentary/interview.
2. Dietrich Bonhoeffer, *Letters and Papers from Prison*, ed. Eberhard Bethge (New York: Macmillan, 1972), 361.

10. 2 Corinthians 12:9

1. Quoted, dated, and discussed in Gerhard O. Forde, *On Being a Theologian of the Cross: Reflections on Luther's Heidelberg Disputation, 1518* (Grand Rapids: Eerdmans, 1997), 62.
2. Tom Junod, "Can You Say . . . Hero?" *Esquire*, November 1998.

11. Psalm 46:10

1. Nicholas Lash, "The Church in the State We're In," *Modern Theology* 13, no. 1 (January 1997): 131.

14. Romans 12:2

1. Bob Pierce quoted in Richard Stearns, *The Hole in the Gospel* (Nashville: Thomas Nelson, 2009), 9.
2. Eugene Peterson, *The Jesus Way* (Grand Rapids: Eerdmans, 2007), 49.

15. John 21:15

1. Maggie Ross, *The Fountain and the Furnace* (Mahwah, NJ: Paulist, 1987), 71.

17. 1 Corinthians 6:19

1. Flannery O'Connor, "A Temple of the Holy Ghost," in *The Complete Stories of Flannery O'Connor* (New York: Farrar, Straus & Giroux, 1971).

20. Jeremiah 29:11

1. Reinhold Niebuhr, *The Irony of American History* (New York: Charles Scribner's Sons, 1952), 63.

21. 1 Samuel 16:7

1. J. R. R. Tolkien, *Fellowship of the Ring* (New York: Ballantine, 1965), 212.

22. Psalm 1:1–2

1. J. Clinton McCann, "Psalms," in *The New Interpreter's Bible* (Nashville: Abingdon, 1996), 4:687.
2. David McCullough, *The Course of Human Events* (New York: Simon & Schuster, 2004), audiobook.

23. Galatians 5:1

1. Natan Sharansky, *Fear No Evil*, trans. Stefani Hoffman (New York: Random House, 1988), 423.
2. Frederick Buechner, *Wishful Thinking: A Seeker's ABC*, rev. ed. (San Francisco: HarperSanFrancisco, 1993), 33.

24. Psalm 98:5–6

1. Walter Brueggemann, *Israel's Praise: Doxology against Idolatry and Ideology* (Philadelphia: Fortress, 1988), 1.
2. Augustine, *On Christian Doctrine*, trans. D. W. Robertson (Indianapolis: Bobbs-Merrill, 1958), 9–10.
3. Robert Coles, *Dorothy Day: A Radical Devotion* (Reading, MA: Addison-Wesley, 1987), 16.

25. Psalm 130:4

1. *Merchant of Venice*, Act IV, scene 1.

26. Matthew 5:9

1. Dietrich Bonhoeffer, *No Rusty Swords*, trans. John Bowden, ed. Edwin Robertson (New York: Harper & Brothers, 1956), 168.
2. Martin Luther King Jr., *Strength to Love* (Philadelphia: Fortress, 1981), 53.
3. Bonhoeffer, *No Rusty Swords*, 168.
4. To learn more about Francis and peacemaking, see my *Conversations with Saint Francis* (Nashville: Abingdon, 2008), chap. 9.

27. Proverbs 16:7

1. Dietrich Bonhoeffer, *No Rusty Swords*, trans. John Bowden, ed. Edwin Robertson (New York: Harper & Row, 1956), 168.

28. 2 Corinthians 9:7

1. Murray Bodo, *Friend of Francis, Fool of God* (Cincinnati: St. Andrew Messenger Press, 1983), 28.
2. Marilynne Robinson, *Gilead* (New York: Farrar, Straus & Giroux, 2004), 31.
3. Thomas Merton, *New Seeds of Contemplation* (New York: New Directions, 1961), 179.

29. Psalm 62:1–2

1. Augustine, *The Confessions of St. Augustine*, trans. John K. Ryan (Garden City, NY: Doubleday, 1960), 44.
2. Lewis B. Smedes, "The Power of Promises," in A *Chorus of Witnesses: Model Sermons for Today's Preacher*, ed. Thomas G. Long and Cornelius Plantinga Jr. (Grand Rapids: Eerdmans, 1994), 156.

30. Hebrews 4:15–16

1. Sue Monk Kidd, *The Secret Life of Bees* (New York: Penguin, 2002), 96f.

31. Exodus 20:9–10

1. Christopher Ringwald, *A Day Apart: How Jews, Christians, and Muslims Find Faith, Freedom, and Joy on the Sabbath* (New York: Oxford University Press, 2007), 24, xi.
2. Annie Dillard, *Holy the Firm* (New York: Harper & Row, 1977), 58.
3. Walter Brueggemann, *Mandate to Difference: An Invitation to the Contemporary Church* (Louisville, KY: Westminster John Knox, 2007), 41.

32. Psalm 119:105

1. George Eliot, *Adam Bede* (New York: Dolphin Books, 1961), 198.

33. James 1:22

1. Richard Bauckham, *James* (New York: Routledge, 1999), 140.

34. Philippians 2:6–7

1. Michael J. Gorman, *Inhabiting the Cruciform God: Kenosis, Justification, and Theosis in Paul's Narrative Soteriology* (Grand Rapids: Eerdmans, 2009), 33, putting a lovely twist on Ernst Käsemann's famous thought that the cross was "the signature of the Risen One."
2. Francis of Assisi, *St. Francis of Assisi: Writings and Early Biographies; English Omnibus of the Sources of the Life of St. Francis*, trans. Raphael Brown, ed. Marion Habig (Chicago: Franciscan Herald Press, 1973), 1448.

35. 1 Samuel 1:15

1. Frederick Buechner, *Wishful Thinking: A Seeker's ABC*, rev. ed. (San Francisco: HarperSanFrancicso, 1993), 120.

37. John 14:6

1. C. S. Lewis, *Mere Christianity* (New York: Macmillan, 1960), 65.

38. Matthew 2:1

1. Dale Allison, *Studies in Matthew* (Grand Rapids: Baker, 2005), 17–41.
2. Dante, *The Divine Comedy: Paradise*, xxxiii, l.145.
3. Benson Bobrick, *The Fated Sky: Astrology in History* (New York: Simon & Schuster, 2005), 79.
4. T. S. Eliot, "Journey of the Magi," in *Collected Poems, 1909–1962* (New York: Harcourt Brace Jovanovich, 1988), 100.

39. Luke 2:34

1. William Wordsworth, "The Virgin," in *The Ecclesiastical Sonnets of William Wordsworth* (New Haven, CT: Yale University Press, 1922), 151.
2. Karl Barth, *Church Dogmatics*, IV/4 (Edinburgh: T. & T. Clark, 1969), 59.
3. Oscar Hijuelos, *Mr. Ives's Christmas* (New York: HarperCollins, 1995), 4.
4. Jean Daniélou, *From Glory to Glory* (Crestwood, NY: St. Vladimir's, 2001), 45f.
5. Søren Kierkegaard, *Purity of Heart Is to Will One Thing*, trans. Douglas V. Steere (New York: Harper & Row, 1938), 53.